PATRIARCHS AND POLITICS

MARILYN WARENSKI

Patriarchs and Politics

THE PLIGHT OF
THE MORMON WOMAN

McGRAW-HILL BOOK COMPANY
New York   St. Louis   San Francisco   Mexico   Toronto   Düsseldorf

Book design by Anita Walker Scott.

Photograph of jailed Mormon leaders courtesy of Zion Book Store, Salt Lake City. Photographs of Ezra Taft Benson, Belle S. Spafford, Barbara Smith, and Spencer W. Kimball, courtesy of Church of Jesus Christ of Latter-day Saints. All other photographs from Utah State Historical Society.

Library of Congress Cataloging in Publication Data

Warenski, Marilyn.
    Patriarchs and politics.
    Bibliography: p.
    Includes index.
    1. Women in Mormonism.   2. Feminism.   I. Title.
BX8641.W373   261.8'34'12   78-17837
ISBN 0-07-068270-4

Published in association with
SAN FRANCISCO BOOK COMPANY

The women's movement is very possibly the greatest single hope for the survival of religious consciousness in the West.

Mary Daly

To accept authority as the source for any theology always runs the risk of providing the answers to questions that are not asked.

Paul Tillich

Contending for the rights of women, my main argument is that if she be not prepared by education to become the companion of man, she will stop the progress of knowledge, for truth must be common to all, or it will be inefficacious with respect to its influence on general practice.

Mary Wollstonecraft

Do you not know that you are (each) an Eve? ... You are the devil's gateway: you are the unsealer of that forbidden tree: you are the first deserter of the divine law: you are she who persuaded him whom the devil was not valiant enough to attack. You destroyed so easily God's image, man. On account of your desert—that is, death—even the Son of God had to die.

Tertullian

For my children
LISA, JANE, JIM, *and* PAUL,
and my husband
JIM

CONTENTS

PREFACE

This book is an examination of women in the Mormon culture from its nineteenth-century beginning to the present time. The text is based on historical research and on the many taped interviews that I conducted with a representative variety of Mormon women, young and old, active and inactive. In a broad sense, however, this study has been my personal exploration of the subject of women in all patriarchal cultures. In the process I have gained an appreciation of the fundamental significance of the philosophy of feminism. From studying the Mormon experience as well as from a review of literature about women in Judaism and traditional Christianity, I increased my awareness of the astonishing anti-female bias that is deeply rooted in and perpetuated by patriarchal religion. This has confirmed for me that the women's rights issues of the twentieth century, however remote from religion they seem, all stem from that bias. In many ways religion has a positive influence upon society, but its subordination of women has been a destructive force. Thus, I have come to view the emergence of feminism and its effort to restructure society as one of the healthiest, most significant social developments to take place in our era.

My interest in researching and writing about Mormon women began to develop in the late 1960s when I was involved in volunteer work at the Utah State Historical Society. In reading old manuscripts and diaries of pioneer Mormon women, I received some first-hand accounts of their experiences from which I was able to gain clearer insight into their thoughts and feelings. It became apparent to me that those accounts frequently did not coincide with the official published histories.

I would like to point out that my decision to investigate the subject of women in the Mormon culture was well under way by the time the Latter-day Saint Church became overtly entangled with the intense political issues of the current women's movement, namely the campaign toward ratification of the Equal Rights Amendment and the International Women's Year meetings. Although I had perceived that the growing resistance of the Mormon patriarchy to the women's movement might ultimately become a matter of public concern, my work on the subject developed independently of, and was not in reaction to, the political controversies that were engendered by the Mormon involvement in those affairs.

My philosophical adventure, which questions the validity of all patriarchal societies, in fact, stems more from my personal experience than from political activism. It might never have occurred had I not returned with my family to Salt Lake City, Utah, in 1962 after living for a decade in New York City. Upon re-entering the LDS culture, of which I am a product, I was reminded—in fact I became painfully aware —of the unusual cultural expectations for women that exist in Mormon country. I was curious about the roots of LDS cultural traditions for women and discovered that some are indeed unique to Mormonism. However, many of the pressures brought to bear on Mormon women are the same as those for women everywhere, but in Mormondom, the set of patriarchal rules and regulations for women is experienced in its most exaggerated form.

In spite of that, I knew from growing up in the Mormon society that the women of my cultural heritage were, by tradition, strong women. I was aware also that the Mormon Church, a male-dominated authoritarian culture in the extreme, claimed to offer its women greater freedom and opportunities than women possess in other cultures. In this interesting cultural paradox, I began to see material for this book.

The strong work ethic in my Mormon background

undoubtedly provided me with the determination and self-discipline to complete this work, but ironically this work has led me to conclusions that are incompatible with Mormonism. Still, it is not my intention to try to convert Mormon women to feminism, nor do I have any interest in instigating a movement toward changing the status of women in the Mormon Church. Knowing the satisfaction of becoming free from patriarchal restraints, it is tempting to become an evangelist for the cause. Nevertheless, if the majority of Mormon women are functioning happily within the system, I have no vested interest in attempting to change that condition. On the other hand, for the many Mormon women who are in personal conflict with the LDS position on women and for those women who feel confined by other patriarchies as well, I hope that this study can be of value. It is also my sincere wish that, through exposure of certain aspects of the Mormon patriarchy, the effectiveness of the concerted efforts of the Mormon Church toward defeat of the national advancement of women will be somewhat diminished. My primary interest, however, has been more academic and philosophical than political.

The warm and friendly atmosphere at the Utah State Historical Society has much to do with my pursuing this book, and to my friends there I am grateful. Historian Dr. Jay Haymond assisted by reading my manuscript, and his interest in promoting oral histories in Utah led to the Historical Society's spon-

soring my interview project by providing the record-
er, tapes, and transcriber. This was of great value to
me, and I hope that the histories and attitudes contained on the tapes will be a useful addition to the
Society's collection. I also appreciate the help of li-
brarian Martha Stewart and of Margaret Lester who
is in charge of the Society's picture collection. Although all the people at the Historical Society do not
necessarily share my feminist point of view, they
never ceased to be accommodating.

I enjoyed the opportunity to become acquainted
with the many interesting Mormon women whom I
interviewed. Their friendliness and cooperation
made my oral history project a special pleasure for
me. My close personal friends also deserve to be
credited for the development of this book. It is from
our many hours of stimulating conversation in which
we shared our ideas and feelings that the creative
thought process was kept alive. My thought development was also aided significantly by the works of
some of the pioneers in the field of feminist philosophy and its relationship to religion. Of these, I would
acknowledge authors Mary Daly and Sheila Collins
in particular.

I owe a special debt of gratitude to Dr. Sterling M.
McMurrin, distinguished professor of philosophy
and Dean of the University of Utah Graduate School.
His book *Theological Foundations of the Mormon
Religion* was a valuable resource for me, and from his
critical evaluation of several of my chapters I received

further benefit of his expertise. For the time he generously expended and for his support, I am appreciative.

Finally, this endeavor that has consumed so much of my time and energy for the past three years could not have been accomplished and enjoyed so completely without the enthusiastic support of my husband Jim. He has read my chapters many times and contributed to them his insight and judgment. He has proved a *helpmate* to me in every way.

M.W.

Salt Lake City
April 1978

1

MORMON WOMAN: SUBSTANCE AND MYTH

Out west in Utah Territory, far from the refinement and sophistication of established Eastern society, there occurred in 1870 a gathering of women the likes of which had not been seen anywhere in America to that time. In a "great indignation mass meeting" held in Salt Lake City, an army of 6,000 Mormon sisters assembled to protest the abuse of female rights

1

in what Mormon historians have called "the most remarkable women's rights demonstration of the age."[1] Exhibiting unusual political expertise for their time, these stalwart sisters of the Mormon Relief Society* dispatched petitions bearing thousands of signatures to the United States Congress requesting their "homestead right" of freedom regarding their marriage style. They also promoted statehood for Utah Territory, and, having acquired the right to female suffrage themselves, these same women out in Mormon country were praised by Mormon historians as having "led the age in that supreme woman's issue."[2]

A century later, in 1977, when women's rights had emerged once more as an important issue of the day, the conscientious Mormon sisters again turned out en masse for many of the International Women's Year meetings which were held throughout the country that year. With Relief Society membership bringing attendance to nearly 14,000, the assemblage for this meeting in lightly populated Utah was twice the size of any other in the United States. Still remarkably unified, the Latter-day Saint women elected from their ranks a slate of delegates who would represent them and the "correct principles" for which they stood at the forthcoming national women's conference. Ironically, however, the Relief Society had completely reversed its position, and, in

*The Relief Society is the women's auxiliary of the Mormon Church.

2

rejecting all of the feminist proposals submitted for consideration by the national women's committee, the Mormon women in 1977 staged one of the greatest anti-feminist demonstrations of our time.

It has long been the pride of the Mormons that the Relief Society, said to be the largest women's organization in the world, has the tradition of uniting in sisterhood to speak out for their rights and to act on their own behalf. In praising the remarkable women of the Mormon culture for their strength, organizational ability, fine character, and exemplary womanhood, Mormon historians have correctly depicted the substance of the Mormon woman, but in describing their tradition of unity as an impressive display of women of Zion* have been orchestrated by the male historians have perpetuated a myth.

Almost without exception the gatherings of the women of Zion* have been orchestrated by the male leaders of the Church, and what often has been labeled erroneously as the powerful force of womanhood has been instead a reflection of the powerful force of the patriarchy. The sisterhood traditionally has raised its unified voice not so much on behalf of women, as is often claimed, but on behalf of the church organization. The activism and cohesiveness achieved by Mormon women in pursuing a common goal is definitely a tribute to the effective Mormon

---

*Zion is defined by Mormons as the dwelling place of the righteous. The state of Utah is designated as Mormon Zion.

system, but neither cause nor method has been rooted in a primary commitment to women. So there seems to be a perplexing and disturbing paradox in the Mormon women of today adopting such an astonishing anti-feminist stand when their pioneer ancestors were united as "feminists," but the situations are more alike than different.

Charges have been heard repeatedly, of course, from the Gentiles* since the early days of the Church that the Saints' women do not think for themselves, and that in blindly following directions of their leaders they "behave like sheep." With consistency and righteous indignation Mormon sisters have denied such accusations. A strong-minded lot, they probably speak the truth when they insist that they are not coerced and that their assertive behavior comes as a result of their own strong convictions. The environment that allows those convictions to develop, however, is created and controlled by the leaders of the Church. The attitudes that are planted, nurtured, and reinforced by the authorities in power generally have been reflected by the Mormon majority. It would be unheard of for the prominent sisters of the Mormon Relief Society to act in defiance of their priesthood leaders.

Feminists would view this type of patriarchal power an obvious deterrent to progress even if it were working to the advantage of women. After all,

*Gentiles are non-Mormons by Mormon definition.

4

they are convinced that patriarchal religious leaders throughout history, purporting to speak the words of their perceived anthropomorphic male God, created the major hurdles for women. There is a strong theoretical assumption among feminist philosophers that those most responsible for woman's unfortunate plight, such as the Apostle Paul and Augustine, have invoked their own *prejudices* as well as *societal trends* of their times in the teachings that have been forever binding on the female sex. But it has been difficult to document a cohesive theory based on ancient history. In the brief history of the Mormon Church, however, feminists can find some outstanding evidence. Within a mere hundred-year span the Mormon patriarchy has demonstrated how woman's "God-given roles" and "His" notion of a woman's sphere can be altered significantly according to the interpretations of men and the needs of society. In fact, in the Mormon experience can be found the ideal case in support of feminism against any patriarchal society.

Early Mormonism presented an example for all to see that when, from necessity, opportunities become available to women, they are capable of accomplishments equal to and sometimes superior to those of men. Then, as the Church progressed, it graphically illustrated the inconsistencies among patriarchal leaders in regard to policies for women, and finally it demonstrated how patriarchal power ultimately and inevitably becomes confining to women in such a

5

system. While feminism certainly can be compatible with organized religion, it is easy to see from the Mormon experience why feminist philosophy is clearly antithetical to patriarchal religion.

As a religion, as a unique American subculture, or as an ethnic group, the Mormons have been a subject of intense curiosity since their dramatic westward trek of the nineteenth century. And their women, having launched their history with a foray into polygamy, still are remembered by some for their involvement in that "scandalous" arrangement.

The Mormon religion was founded in 1830 by Joseph Smith, a young man living in Palmyra, New York, and it is grounded in the revelations he claimed to have received. At a time of religious instability in America, Joseph had become confused by the religious controversies in his area. He reported that two personages, the Father and Son, appeared before him while he was praying for inspiration and counseled him against accepting the tenets of any of the existing religious denominations. According to Mormon history, the subsequent revelations of this New York farm boy guided him to a set of golden plates buried in a hill nearby. On the plates was written the history of the early people on the North American continent, said to be the lost tribe of Israel.

The plates provided the basis for Mormon doctrine, but it was further developed and refined through the regular, continuing revelations of the Prophet. Smith was a charismatic personality and he started his work at a time of extensive religious experimentation, so the new religion readily acquired a following. Each convert no doubt had a fascinating individual story to tell, but whatever motivated the original Saints, whether it was a search for truth, for a better way of life, or for romance or adventure, they certainly gained the adventure, and more than they could have bargained for.

Called upon through revelation to establish a Zion in America, the prophet Smith led the new band first to Kirtland, Ohio, but, experiencing economic disaster and intense unpopularity there, they soon moved on to Missouri. They were driven from several towns in that "new land of promise" after antagonizing the natives each time with their unusual habits, their separateness and tendency to vote as a bloc, and their claim of divine right to the land. Still the Saints increased in number all the while. Determined to endure, they re-crossed the Mississippi and retreated into Illinois only to repeat their negative experiences there. But this time, with added rumors about plural marriage in their camp, the hostility toward them resulted in Joseph Smith and his brother Hyrum being attacked by an angry mob from Nauvoo and shot to death.

It was providential, perhaps, that upon the martyring of their Prophet, the Saints should have had among them the likes of a Brigham Young. One of the most gifted and powerful leaders in American history, Young quickly won the confidence of these downtrodden, persecuted people. It was said, in fact, that as he spoke he even took on the aura of the Prophet Joseph. Leaving some splinter groups behind, the majority of Mormons then abandoned their struggles with hostile Americans, and following Brigham Young westward, launched their war with the elements.

Their mass migration from Illinois to the new land of Utah and their making that desert "blossom as a rose" required not only a liberal amount of survival instinct but almost incredible creative energy and dedication, comparable to that of the cathedral builders of Europe. Geographically isolated from the familiarity of past lives in New England, the Middle West, the British Isles, or Scandinavia, these converts now had only each other and their religion. Under the guidance of their astute leader they organized into communities rather than spreading out, and when conflicts resumed with Gentile Americans unity became their trademark.

It must be emphasized that the Saints involved in this historical episode were not all male Saints. Women were there too. In fact, women were there in almost equal number shouldering an equal share of the burdens. Historians generally have been negligent in giving due recognition to the contributions of women, but the current surge of national interest has sent waves of researchers back to historical documents to extract the bits and pieces of women's history. Because the Mormons have valued record-keeping from the beginning, the stories of the extraordinary pioneer Mormon women are told in the abundance of diaries and journals they kept. Many of these writings are readily accessible to the public and they provide a veritable gold mine for the history buff. Even if comparable records were available, it is doubtful that any women's history could be more impressive or thought-provoking. As Wallace Stegner wrote in his book *Gathering of Zion*, "Their women were incredible."

If the current status of Mormon women presents a paradox, various interpretations, distortions and half-truths have made their entire history seem one of paradox. When Mormon polygamous wives were pitied in other parts of the country as poor victims of male oppression, those wives rose up in defense of polygamy, and while Gentiles were imagining them as household drudges and slaves, the women out in Utah Territory were realizing many of the feminists' goals. With no doors closed to them regarding work, they were participating in almost every business and profession known to man. In fact, the unusual concentration of women physicians in Utah Territory in the late nineteenth century eventually caused males to complain of "petticoat domination" of the medical profession. And it was the "unsophisticated" Mormon women from the western frontier who charged in the 1870s that Victorian ideals regarding women were wasteful of human potential and demeaning to women.

The most prominent heroines of Mormon history, even if only a fraction of the accounts of their accomplishments are true, give cause for contemplation. In no way could they be classified as ordinary. There was the revered Mormon midwife Patty Sessions who, at her death at ninety-nine, was said to have assisted with 3,977 births.[3] All across the plains into Utah, traveling by foot or horseback, often through blizzards in the night, Mother Sessions was relied upon to "put the women to bed." She also raised her own flock of children and cared for a chronically ailing husband. Patty was only one of many early Mormon midwives who not only brought new Saints into the world, but frequently guarded the health of entire communities as well.

The need to replace the aging midwives brought such women as Dr. Ellis Shipp into the forefront. Ellis, a plural wife, was mother of four small children when she went off to Women's Medical College in Pennsylvania in 1875. Journeying back and forth to visit her children and husband left behind in Utah, and working part-time all the while to augment her meager home allowance, she delivered her fifth child the day after her last examination of her second medical school year.[4] With her hard-earned medical education, Ellis gave a lifetime of service as a physician and teacher among the Mormons.

For Dr. Martha Hughes Cannon, another plural wife, earning a medical degree was only the beginning of her achievements. In 1897 Martha went on to become the first woman in the United States to serve as a state senator, defeating her own husband for the honor.[5] On the subject of political firsts for women, Utah claimed another in 1912 when the widow Mary Howard of Kanab, Utah, was elected the first woman mayor in America.

Every Mormon woman has grown up with stories of the pioneer stalwart Eliza R. Snow. Plural wife of both Joseph Smith and Brigham Young, she was close enough to the power to be power herself. As the right hand of the partriarchy Eliza applied her executive ability in the organizing of church auxiliaries, serving as president of the Mormon Relief Society for thirty years. With her breeding and literary background from the East, she was said to have been "a woman with a good mind" and was well known as a poet among her people.

If Eliza R. Snow is the most prominent of the early role models, Brigham Young's daughter, Susa Young Gates, is for many the historical favorite. This artistic mother of thirteen was a prolific writer, musician, teacher, and suffragist. Having traveled internationally, she established a reputation as a gracious hostess for important visitors to Utah as well. There are indications that in her younger years Susa, caught up in the suffragist movement at the turn of the century, had the spirit of a genuine rebel. However, with age she too bowed to conformity and ultimately became one of the leading devotees of the Church. Even before Susa's involvement with suf-

11

frage there were the original Utah activists such as Sarah Kimball, who incorporated her political and suffrage activities into her church work, and Emmeline B. Wells, who attended national suffrage meetings and cultivated friendships with none other than national leaders Susan B. Anthony and Elizabeth Cady Stanton. For many years Emmeline, a plural wife of Salt Lake City mayor Daniel H. Wells, was editor-in-chief of the splendid Mormon sisters' newspaper *The Woman's Exponent.*

While many of these notable women were thrust into prominence by virtue of their close relationships with the patriarchy and enjoyed servants and a surprising number of privileged-class advantages, considering Mormon frontier life, there were countless obscure sisters who were no less remarkable. Both individually and as a group, the early women of the Mormon culture were, of necessity, courageous, competent, hard-working women whose contributions were vital to the success of the Mormon kingdom. In fact, just reading about the seemingly endless activities of such high-principled achievers can be overwhelming, but there is comfort in knowing that they had the reinforcement of a supportive community and often went about the serious business of living with an element of good cheer and a salty brand of humor, vestiges of which are found in the corners of rural Utah.

They had many characteristics in common, but, with their variety of backgrounds, of course these

12

nineteenth-century Mormon women were not all alike. Because they were influenced by the attitudes of the patriarchy, there were trends in their thinking patterns, however, and from their beautifully articulated statements there is little doubt that one trend in the nineteenth century was toward a genuine commitment to the principle of woman's suffrage. For many Mormon women that commitment grew into full and enthusiastic support of equal rights for women. But were they feminists?

In his book *Women of Mormondom* (1877), Latter-day Saint historian Edward Tullidge apparently answers a critical and suspicious public regarding the women's rights activities of the nineteenth-century Mormon sisters when he explains, "The acts and examples of franchised Mormon women are not the acts and promptings of President Brigham Young and his apostles, but of the leaders of the sisterhood."[6] Only incidentally does Tullidge make this important addition: "It may be stated however, that President Young and the apostles approved and blessed their doings, and that confesses much to their honor."[7] Anyone with even a casual acquaintance with the Mormon culture, then or now, would assume that had these women's activities not been endorsed, declared righteous, and promoted by the patriarchy, they never would have occurred.

So convinced of the righteousness of polygamy were Mormon patriarchal authorities at that time that when its legality was challenged by Gentile Americans they encouraged the political demonstrations by women in defense of that basic "woman's right." Indeed, Mormon leaders *required* the women to support the principle of polygamy or leave the Church. To allow some of the less fortunate sisters in the state the opportunity to attend the giant *women's rights* mass meetings in Salt Lake City, the fare was reduced on the church-owned railroad to defray their travel expenses. With that kind of encouragement the Mormon women of the nineteenth century rose up as defenders of women's rights in splendid fashion.

When compared with the political demonstrations of the Mormon sisterhood a century ago then, the performance of Mormon women at such events as the International Women's Year meetings of 1977 clearly presents a parallel instead of a paradox. While official statements to the media consistently denied any interference in that meeting by the Mormon patriarchy, it is a well-known and documented fact that the participation of the Mormon Relief Society was endorsed, if not instigated, by a leading church authority whose right-wing political leanings and attitudes about current women's issues had been made very clear to the membership.

A letter was circulated through the Relief Societies of the state inviting their participation in the conference. It began, "This is a follow-up of the telephone call you received from President Ezra Taft Benson's office, and here is what should be done." The Society's leaders claimed that instead of Benson promot-

14

ing their action they had sought his permission. Whatever triggered the giant Relief Society operation that summoned ten members from each ward* in the state and brought 14,000 women together, the leaders insisted that the women were not told how to vote, but simply were advised to support "correct principles." Still, when people connected with the conference began receiving calls from duty-bound Mormon sisters asking, "Where is it we are supposed to go?," they should have been warned that an unusual event was about to take place.

Even Relief Society officers claimed to have been astonished by the intensity of the event. Regardless of the fact that it had happened before, they had not anticipated that militant right-wing Mormon activists would so effectively "plug in" to the church organizational system and exploit it to their own advantage. Again, the climate that allowed such an effective merger of conservative politics with the Mormon Relief Society had been firmly established long before by the politically oriented patriarchy. If not articulated, the "correct principles" were assumed because today, the right-wing position *is* the Church position.

No longer contained in a remote territory of the American West, the Mormon Church has grown into a sizable worldwide empire, and its Relief Societies have been mobilized against the women's

---

*A ward is a neighborhood church.

15

movement throughout the country. Repeating their Utah strategy as a highly organized anti-feminist bloc, the Mormon sisters turned out at the 1977 International Women's Year meetings in other states, garnering in some the majority of delegate votes for the national women's meeting. It is no coincidence that many of the delegates elected, like the Mormon women's rights leaders of yesterday, were Relief Society officers and wives of Mormon officials. Confident now of their righteousness in opposing the women's rights movement they once endorsed with equal zeal, the Mormon patriarchy is committed to helping that righteousness prevail throughout the land.

Unlike women of other organized religions and religious denominations, Mormon women have always presented an image of unity. The Mormon Relief Society is structured so that thousands of the sisters can be activated on a moment's notice. The Society stands ready at all times to speak the voice of the Church and the majority view. However, Mormon women always have been more diversified than their collective image suggests. A substantial segment of the sisterhood in the 1970s has felt betrayed by the aggressive anti-feminist behavior of their group, expressing emotions that have ranged from mild disappointment to outrage. In Mormondom, where "nothing is long ago,"* the total reversal of a

*Nothing Is Long Ago is a novel about Mormon Utah by Virginia Sorenson.

16

trend within a century left some Mormon women with an understandably confused self-image. With the traditions established by their hardy grandmothers still very much a part of their lives, many have attempted to perpetuate the platform of Mormonism *and* feminism on which their ancestors stood. These women deplore the change in their sisterhood, but the change they think they see actually is no change at all. If the current anti-feminist actions of the Mormon majority have seemed to contradict their past, in their unchanging devotion to an everchanging patriarchy the behavior of Mormon women has been both consistent and predictable. In this confusing Mormon drama the only change that has occurred is in those few Mormon women who have questioned the judgment of the patriarchy and have shown allegiance instead to their Mormon heritage and feminist traditions (if only an illusion) of the past.

In the early days or at the present time, to be a Mormon and a feminist at the same time would require considerable compromise of either feminist or religious principles. In the extensive number of taped interviews I have conducted regarding the current status of Mormon women,[8] that dichotomy was ever-present, creating its inevitable conflicts. Without the power to alter church policies they consider truly regrettable, many women in this authoritarian patriarchal system have found themselves out of step with modern society. By remorsefully wishing for

17

church authorities to return to a more liberal interpretation of the woman's sphere, they dramatize the very essence of the problem: obviously, those who must ask for their freedom don't have it—and, in this case, they have the added burden of extreme guilt about asking. While it has been a proud tradition of Mormonism that "the women in the Church have been given opportunities that others don't have," those privileges are always in jeopardy, as history has demonstrated. As is said in regard to life, "The Lord giveth and the Lord taketh away," so it has been with the patriarchal representatives of the Lord in regard to women's roles.

Because of its doctrine of continuing revelation, the Mormon Church has not been altogether confined by the teachings of the apostles and early prophets as has been the case with some of the more traditional religions. Nevertheless, Mormon authorities have shown how, in their official capacities as prophets, they could sanction polygamy and then condemn it, and could praise women of the Church as feminist leaders when it served the needs of the Church and then reject any association with feminism. The dictionary innocuously defines feminism as "the theory of the political, economic, and social equality of the sexes, or the organized activity on behalf of women's rights and interests," but as feminism became a major social reform cause and threatened their system the Mormon patriarchy chose to define it as evil.

18

One of the most significant social developments of our times, the current battle for women's equality was rooted in legitimate injustice and given momentum by the anger of its leaders. The goals of the women's movement were misunderstood by many, however, as it became identified primarily with irrational and often destructive actions of radical elements whose broad variety of interests distorted the fundamental issues. As one facetious male supporter observed, "Feminism won't be taken seriously as a philosophy until it is taken out of the hands of hysterical women." Unfortunately, progress toward social reform rarely is accomplished without the radical behavior of the angry oppressed bringing the problems into public focus, but after the current feminist disruption has subsided, the women's movement most assuredly will be viewed as a major enhancement of human dignity. Progress toward freedom and human rights could not be assessed as evil.

In reacting to the social upheaval the women's movement has wrought, authorities of the Mormon Church have voiced their loudest objections on the issues of sexual freedom, homosexuality, abortion, and destruction of the family. In the opinion of theologian and philosopher Mary Daly, to concentrate on such issues is to overlook the essential point. Moving beyond definition toward a serious philosophy of feminism, Daly, in her book *Beyond God the Father*, contends that the above subjects, while

19

related to feminism, are not necessarily feminist issues.[9] That is, a woman could be feminist without endorsing any of those ideas. According to Daly's philosophy, a feminist could be opposed to marriage or totally committed to motherhood and traditional marriage; she could believe in sexual freedom or sexual restraint; she could adhere to a conception of deity or she might not believe in any God; but putting on the line the "gut issue" of feminism, it would be impossible to be a feminist without believing that women must be responsible for their own decisions.

Religious women of Western society have been intimidated into submission through the centuries by the decisions of patriarchal religious leaders, but those leaders could not logically know or assume that without the guidance and discipline of their male ecclesiastic power, women, in making their own decisions, would behave in an irresponsible manner. Can it be that the Mormon patriarchy of today, in its vigorous resistance to the feminist movement, has not missed the essential point—indeed that it has a better grasp of the movement's fundamental issue than it has led the public to believe? Certainly, the male authorities of the Latter-day Saint Church must be profoundly aware that unless Mormon women reject their patriarchal system there can be no such thing as a Mormon feminist.

Sir, a woman preaching is like a dog's walking on his hind legs. It is not done well; but you are surprised that it is done at all.

Samuel Johnson

2

WOMAN AND THE PRIESTHOOD

The complex relationship of women to the Mormon priesthood can be understood best when compared to the involvement of women with the priesthood in other religions. Among churches of the world, of course, associating women with the priesthood had been uncommon, if not rare, before the emergence of the women's movement in the 1960s. But with the new wave of feminism focusing on leadership power in previously male-dominated institutions, anything less than the authority of the priest-

21

hood in religious organizations would fall short of the feminist goal.

There are a few feminist philosophers who take the more radical position that acquiring priesthood could accomplish little on behalf of the feminist movement. Mary Daly, for instance, while recognizing the patriarchy as the source of women's inequality, asserts in *Beyond God the Father* that the traditional patriarchal system, which was authored by males for the benefit of males, is so hopelessly sexist that any attempt by women to be assimilated into such a system would be self-defeating. Objecting to the common assumption that God is a male, vocal feminists who share Daly's point of view suggest that religious systems must be totally redefined. In religions of antiquity, they remind us, the holy spirit was conceived as feminine. They also emphasize that philosophical systems, with the exception of theology, do not have a masculine and feminine.

Nevertheless, many women who have considered themselves feminists haven't entertained ideas of overthrowing entire church structures. More traditional in a religious sense and of a less revolutionary nature, such women began by concentrating on gaining a fair share of the leadership. No longer, they decided, could all women be happy simply mending the altar cloths while men carried on the priestly functions at the altar, nor should they continue cooking church suppers and raising funds while the men made all the important decisions. Their progress was unimpressive at first, amounting to a variety of token gains, but those gains were considerably easier for some than others.

Highest on the scale of progress toward achieving women's goals are the liberal Protestant denominations. With no doctrinal interpretations prohibiting such actions, over eighty denominations had begun ordaining women into the ministry by 1975. It is significant that these groups rarely use the term "priesthood," having rejected the Catholic conception of the word at the time of their separation from the Roman Church. Ordination of women was viewed as "a natural step for the Church to take" by the United Presbyterians of the United States who, in accepting that philosophy in the late 1950s, preceded the women's movement by a decade. Many Protestants today share the attitude that because churches are naturally concerned with human development, they should lead the way in correcting such injustices as race and sex discrimination. In denominations where awareness and self-discovery are emphasized, the current women's movement, in fact, was readily incorporated as an important part of church life.

It must be acknowledged, however, that, while many denominations began accepting women into the ministry, only 5 per cent of the Protestant churches could claim by the mid-1970s that they had women in senior ministerial posts, which demonstrates that even in such liberal groups tradition dies hard. Social

23

acceptance of a woman as principal minister was the major obstacle, with resistance often coming from women members themselves who had been conditioned to feel more comfortable with a father figure in the ministry. But a 1975 report from the National Council of Churches confirms that, after initial skepticism, churches that open their pulpits to women discover they make excellent ministers. Natural "feminine" qualities such as openness and the capacity for caring and nurturing, ironically the very qualities cited by church fathers as proof that woman's God-given roles are mother and homemaker, have been shown to be especially suitable for the ministry as well.

Women made progress also in the synagogues of reformed Judaism, where they have slowly gained acceptance as spiritual leaders despite the strong undertow of prejudice against them that prevails in that culture. By the middle of the 1970s there were several women rabbis in America and an increasing number were entering into rabbinical training. Then, in a further departure from the Jewish male tradition, the privilege to participate in bar mitzvah was extended to young Jewish girls. "Operatively, women's participation in Judaism, as in other religions, has been anything but ennobling," said Rabbi Abner Bergman of Congregation Kol Ami in Salt Lake City, speaking to a group of university women. He explained that the tradition of the male rabbi no doubt was established in the beginning simply out of biological circumstances. Because women were kept occupied bearing and raising children, only the men had the freedom to pursue scholarship and the intellectual life required of a rabbi. Noting that Judaism is indeed conservative, Rabbi Bergman said that it is also humanly developmental. "Therefore, it now encourages the changing status of women which," he emphasized, "is not in conflict with the scriptures."

Within the Episcopal Church there was strong support for women who in the 1960s launched their campaign for leadership positions, but there was great resistance as well. In this church that partly bridges the gap between liberal Protestantism and traditional Catholicism, women were permitted to train for the ministry to serve in assistant capacities, but they were denied the priesthood, the true leadership of the church. For the Episcopal Church, ordaining women to the priesthood was a more complex matter, and for several years much public attention was focused on the dramatic struggle of eleven women ministers to achieve that goal. Those opposing the movement objected primarily on historical grounds, reasoning that because the Lord chose only men as apostles it would be in keeping with His plan to maintain that tradition. Of course, others who supported women's ordination disagreed with that assumption, arguing that the early situation of Christianity should be viewed in the context of the times and not be binding today. They noted that slavery also was practiced in early times, but as the Church grew in wisdom, the Holy Spirit guided the members to examine such practices just as it now guides them to broaden their view of the ministry. Vigorous protests from some Episcopal clergymen were interpreted by feminists as demonstrating that men in the hierarchy are far more concerned about pomp, power, and tradition than about correcting existing equalities.

After extensive debate, the Episcopal Church General Convention of September 1976 finally voted in favor of ordaining women into the priesthood and made the necessary changes to accommodate them. This issue, along with several others, resulted in the organization of a variety of splinter groups such as the Anglican Church of North America, and echoes of the divisive controversy no doubt will be heard for years to come, but the affirmative vote was considered by many as a major victory, not only for the women ministers involved, but for women everywhere.

One authority who did not view the decision of the Episcopal Church with favor was Pope Paul VI, who pronounced that "it created a grave obstacle for the cause of ecumenism." The Roman Catholic Church, along with the Eastern Orthodox Church and various fundamentalist and evangelical groups, remains at the bottom of the scale in terms of accepting women as leaders. Pope Paul had made his position clear earlier with the statement he issued to the Committee for International Women's Year in April 1975:

Although women do not receive the call to the apostolate for the Twelve and therefore to the ordained ministry, they are, none the less, invited to follow Christ as disciples and co-workers.[1]

But feminists in Catholicism, a small but vocal minority, were by no means intimidated by this discouraging message. Insisting that the issue must be faced by the Church, they continued their drive for ordaining women into the priesthood, drawing well over a thousand enthusiasts to the Catholic Women's Conference held in Detroit in November 1975. In a session entitled "Priesthood Now: A Call to Action," one of the many nuns in attendance expressed her opinion that ordination of women would not change the character of the Roman Catholic mass, which is based on a model over two thousand years old. As reported by the Associated Press, those at the conference who aspired to the ordained ministry were asked to stand to acknowledge their hope, and the others blessed that sizable group by making the sign of the cross.

Explaining that they didn't want to "mislead" the women by remaining silent on the issue, the Most Reverend Joseph L. Bernardin of the National Con-

27

ference of Catholic Bishops responded to their assertive behavior with this policy statement:

The constant tradition and practice of the Catholic Church
against ordination of women, interpreted (whenever interpreted) as divine law, is of such a nature as to consti-
tute a clear teaching of the Ordinary Magisterium of the
Church. Though not formally defined, this is Catholic
doctrine.[2]

Catholic leaders draw upon the teachings of Saint
Paul, Saint Thomas Aquinas, and Saint Augustine in
defending the traditional patriarchal position which
designates men as leaders and women as mothers and
homemakers. As in the Episcopal Church, the validity of applying these teachings in today's society is a
debated issue. However, the Catholic Church is not a
democracy. Only the Pope, acting in conjunction
with the bishops of the world, could authorize
women in the priesthood, and that change could not
occur until Catholic scholars conclude an exhaustive
study of Divine Revelation to determine that such an
ordination is possible. It is significant to note, however, that in the 1970s several appointed commis-
sions within the Catholic Church have launched the
academic research on the subject, but the willingness
of the Catholic Church to study the issue can in no
way be interpreted to mean that ordination of
women is imminent. In fact, according to Cardinal
Timothy Manning, spiritual leader of two million
American Catholics, "Women seeking the priest-

hood in the Roman Catholic Church are beating against a rock."[3]

It is evident, even from this brief account of their activities, that a slow-growing but significant trend is developing among women in organized religion. By comparison then, let us consider the progress of women in the Mormon Church. While it is true that Mormonism is considered a fundamentalist religion where literal interpretation of the Bible prevents change from occurring readily, the elevated place of women in the Church has been a source of great pride to the Mormons. They have boasted that their progressive attitudes toward women have been far in advance of those of other churches. On the status of Mormon women, Thomas O'Dea stated in his book *The Mormons* (1957):

While plural marriage is the aspect of Mormon life that has become best known to outsiders, it is nevertheless an important fact to note that Mormonism early came very close to accepting the equality of women with men.[4]

O'Dea goes on to explain that, although they have accepted patriarchal ideals of family organization, Mormons always have recognized that women are not basically inferior to men and he cited early suffrage in Utah as an expression of that attitude. Can it be assumed then that Mormon women are rapidly gaining positions of leadership in the Church? Nothing could be further from the truth.

If Catholic women are beating against a rock, Mormon women are hiding under it. Because of a theology which Mormon scholar Sterling M. McMurrin describes as "a unique and uneasy union of nineteenth-century liberalism with fourth-century Christian fundamentalism,"[5] Mormon women in a changing society find themselves locked into a paradoxical situation. Among women in religious organizations their early elevated position might have been enviable, but the essential present-day feminist goals of priesthood and leadership are apparently out of the question for the sisters of the Mormon Church. In responding to a question on the subject, none of the Mormon women I interviewed expected to see such a radical development in the Church, and even those who believed in women's leadership considered the pursuit a futile one. A surprising number of women, attempting to brush off the question with humor, responded with statements like "Who would want the priesthood! It would only mean more work!" But by far the most common reaction to the idea of priesthood for Latter-day Saint women was the remark "It could not occur in my lifetime." Slightly aghast at the thought of a female priesthood, one woman expressed the opinion that "the Church will grow and change and develop, but the system will never permit change to that degree."[6]

Before discussing the various obstacles that prevent Mormon women from holding the priesthood,

30

we must recognize an extraordinary feature of the Mormon religion. In the Latter-day Saint Church, which has a lay clergy, the priesthood is not confined to its leaders but is extended to virtually all male members of the Church (except Blacks). Needless to say, this has far-reaching consequences for women. The issue of their gaining the priesthood would not be applicable only to a small group seeking leadership of the Church, but would involve all women in the Mormon culture.

As we examine further why Mormon women cannot hold the priesthood, it must be noted that they often speak as if they do hold it. This discrepancy exists because of the notion that women enjoy the "blessings" of the priesthood vicariously through their husbands, and also because of the Mormon custom of calling women's traditional "God-given roles" their "priesthood duties" or "priesthood callings." In frequently neglecting to make the distinction between such callings and the actual priesthood, Church leaders over the years have engaged in a kind of double-talk on the subject. For instance, when the question is posed, "Do women have the priesthood?," some Mormons would agree with the answer of the third Mormon president, John Taylor, who said in 1879, "Yes, in connection with their husbands," hastening to add, "but the husband is the head."[7] On the other hand, others would accept the opinion of Charles Penrose of the Church First

31

Presidency who in 1921 answered an emphatic no to that question. He explained:

Sisters have said to me sometimes, "But I hold the priesthood with my husband." "Well," I asked, "what office do you hold?" Then they could not say much more. . . .it (the priesthood) does not belong to them; they cannot do that properly any more than they can change into a man."[8]

Of course, women could have received a misimpression about their status from Brigham Young himself when he made such statements as "The man that honors his Priesthood and the woman that honors her Priesthood will receive an everlasting inheritance."[9] But woman's position is placed in proper perspective by Latter-day Saint theologian Rodney Turner in his book *Woman and the Priesthood* (1972), simply from the way he writes about women's "priesthood duties" with quotation marks and of men's Priesthood with a capital P.

It is interesting that many Mormon women who are active in the feminist movement accept their position in the church patriarchal system while demanding power for women in secular government. An inquiry about this inconsistency elicits a defensive response from some women, who explain that they are faithful to the church doctrine of the priesthood because it comes directly from revelation and is believed to be God's system. Revelation means the Mormon belief in modern-day revelation, the aspect of the religion that is cited by the majority of Mormon women as the primary reason they cannot hold the priesthood.

When controversy arises on this subject, support for Mormon doctrine is centered on biblical teachings, as in other religions, but additionally it is based on the nineteenth-century revelations of Joseph Smith. Because those revelations also call for an all-male priesthood, they confirm for Mormons the validity of the sex-role designations of Paul and the prophets of the Old Testament. If contemporary society requires a re-evaluation of those roles, Mormons expect that to be revealed to the current President and Prophet of the Church.

Participants in a group discussion explained to me that for them it is not a question of challenging the right of the church as an institution to have an all-male priesthood, but a question of challenging what is alleged to be and what they as Latter-day Saints have to accept. "Even if women have a problem reconciling such a thing as an all-male priesthood, questioning the Church position is not something they can do," one woman argued. "That would be like saying, 'I have as much revelatory power as the Prophet, and therefore, I will challenge him on this point.'"

An active feminist but currently inactive Mormon added this comment: "In other words, if you entertain such an heretical thought you would no longer have faith in revelatory power and you would probably be far enough away from the Church to step out of the system, which is what I had to do." Again, employing humor to deal with a delicate subject, another member of the group quipped, "And at that point, if you didn't step out, you would be pushed out."[10] Couched in humor but rooted in fear, her statement alluded to a significant problem which was more explicitly described in another taped interview with a woman who said, "I can see a woman wondering why she shouldn't have the priesthood. I can understand women thinking that in their heads, but I have never been able to imagine women asking for the priesthood without asking to be excommunicated."[11]

Mormon sisters are cautious indeed about discussing priesthood for women. In fact, even when women's rights advocates speak of improving their status in the Church, the subject of priesthood is conspicuously avoided. While Catholic women continue to campaign actively toward that goal in spite of the Pope's objections, the majority of Mormon women are reluctant even to raise the issue.

If a system which accepts modern-day revelation and gives prophet status to its male authorities makes the priesthood seem inaccessible to women, the nature of some of the revelations provides additional major obstacles. According to those revelations, not only should the priesthood be all-male, but, as previously noted, all Mormon males should hold the priesthood, the power of which they are to exercise as patriarchal head of the family as well as in church leadership positions. And the Mormon view of the patriarchal family, set forth in their unique doctrine of "eternal marriage," would create a serious complication for women seeking the priesthood.

In adopting the patriarchal family structure, Mormonism is not unusual among religions, but it departs from traditional Christianity in its belief that the family unit extends beyond the grave into an eternal world. The contract of the Mormon temple marriage "seals" a man and woman together "for time and all eternity," which means that they will be able to dwell, with their children, in the kingdom of God forever. Progress toward this eternal paradise is uppermost in the minds of Mormons, who view their life on earth as the necessary step between their pre-existent and eternal worlds. Therefore, it always has been considered a primary duty of the Saints to marry and produce as many children as possible, thus providing bodies for the spirits waiting in the pre-existence to be born.

For Mormons, eternal salvation in the kingdom of God must be earned, so they must work toward perfection while on earth. This aspect of the doctrine will be further discussed in the following chapter, but its importance as it relates to Mormon priesthood must be mentioned here. Through possession of the priesthood, a Mormon male is justified in assuming presidency over his family and he should righteously exercise that privilege. By blessing his family with spiritual guidance, each Mormon male can become God-like, and by authority of his priesthood, he shall continue to rule over his individual kingdom throughout eternity. Of this opportunity, Rodney Turner writes:

Can God be distinguished from his attributes? Are they not as one? Can any man become as God unless he internalizes the Holy Priesthood which has been bestowed upon him? . . .Those, like Jesus, who perfect the faith, do not simply *hold* the Priesthood, they *are* the Priesthood. (Italics supplied.)[12]

For a woman, the ultimate reward is to join her husband in the kingdom of God and to share in the blessings of his priesthood. And this she can achieve by fulfilling her obligations to the Church and serving as a mother and a helpmate to the best of her ability. It is significant in Mormonism that although each "spirit" is valued and should progress toward salvation individually, only the married can enter into the highest glory which the Mormons call the Celestial Kingdom. Therefore, in this partnership of mutual obligations and mutual rewards, Mormon men and women are dependent upon each other for exaltation. If, in this exalted state, the rewards seem unevenly distributed, the appropriateness of the arrangement is nevertheless constantly stressed by Church leaders.

Brigham Young's counselor Heber C. Kimball advised women not to resent the priesthood privileges of men that they themselves cannot possess, and suggested by the following admonition that the early Saints had trouble with some of the sisters of the kingdom about accepting the situation:

Do not go round talking about your husband and talking against the Priesthood you are connected to. I do not say many of you do it, but you that do it are poor, miserable skunks.[13]

And reminiscent of the words of Paul, Brigham Young told the women:

Respect the power of the Priesthood while it is upon your husbands. Women have not the degree of light and knowledge that their husbands have, and they have not the power over their passions.[14]

Thus, the traditional teachings of the Bible regarding sex roles have been repeated throughout the history of the Mormon Church to reinforce the unusual marriage doctrine that came to them through revelation.

It is easy to see that if a Mormon woman asked for the priesthood, she would not be making a simple request for a leadership position of the Church. She would be interfering with the patriarchal family structure on earth, not to mention altering the entire Mormon conception of eternity. There is no question that to be offered such advantages as the security of marriage and children for eternity plus a share in the blessings of the priesthood was considered progressive doctrine on behalf of women in the nineteenth century. In other religions, women were rarely given so much consideration. But ironically, that nineteenth-century Mormon doctrine, so far ahead of its time by putting women in close proximity to "priesthood blessings," now keeps them far away from the priesthood itself, today within the reach of women in many other religious organizations. By accepting that doctrine as it now stands, Mormon women continue to accept the compromise of limited roles and subordinate positions to men while on earth in exchange for a promise, not of the priesthood, but of the blessings of their husbands' priesthood in the eternal world. This is what the late philosopher Waldemer P. Read called "staking it all on the tar-paper shack in the sky."[15]

Another obstacle to Mormon women acquiring the priesthood can be found in the meaning of the word itself. Providing a key, the dictionary gives two definitions of priesthood: one, the office, dignity, or character of a priest; and two, the whole body of priests. Liberal Protestants would find the second definition appropriate. For them, individuals who are authorized to perform the sacred rites of the church make up the priesthood, or the ministry. However, Mormons conceive the priesthood to be something different and more significant. Here, the

Mormon position is similar to that of the Catholics, both of which correspond better to the first dictionary definition. That a certain elusiveness is connected with the word in Mormon society was indicated by a woman who said, "I'm not sure what priesthood means, but I know it's not something I can have."

In his book *Theological Foundations of the Mormon Religion*, Sterling M. McMurrin presents an interesting discussion of the meaning of priesthood, explaining the Mormon and Catholic views in terms of the universals of Platonism. Reviewing the metaphysics involved, he describes the nature of a universal as it relates to a particular which has existence in space and time. A white object is a particular, but whiteness is a universal; a human being is a particular, but humanity is a universal; just acts and true statements are particulars, while justice and truth are universals. In what McMurrin calls his most significant philosophical contribution, Plato maintained that universals are real entities instead of just words used to describe particular things. That is to say, they have an independent existence. For instance, truth is real and eternal, beauty and goodness are real and eternal, and these impersonal absolutes are the foundation structure of the universe.

In Platonism there was no living God, but McMurrin explains that as the developing Christian theology began incorporating Greek metaphysics, the personal God of the Hebrews came to be described in

39

terms of Greek universals. Then truth, beauty, and goodness were thought to be real and eternal because they were real absolutes in the mind of the living God. From the careful study of universals by their theologians, the Catholic Church, "sophisticated in philosophical matters," accepted the Platonic doctrine of universals in much of its philosophy, applying it in the conception of priesthood.

On the other hand, the Mormon Church, whose doctrine was said to have been revealed instead of derived from metaphysical principles, never developed a specific theory of universals. Nevertheless, in frequently referring to "eternal laws" and "eternal principles," Mormons obviously assumed the reality of universals, indicating some acquaintance with those ideas. For instance, they speak and write as if "church" were a universal, even though no official doctrine defines it as such. While "The Church" of the Mormons is quite different from "The Church" of the Catholics, both conceive it to be absolute and eternal. In contrast, most Protestants simply associate the church with its active membership.

The status of priesthood as a universal, however, is not merely suggested in Mormonism. It is one word that is quite explicitly described in the doctrine in those terms. Joseph Smith said, "The Priesthood is an everlasting principle, and existed with God from eternity, and will to eternity, without beginning of days or end of years."[16] Regarding Smith's definition, it should be noted that, unlike the Catholic

40

view, it is characteristic for Mormon universals to be
described as existing independently of God, much
like those of early Platonism. That priesthood has the
character of a universal has been imprinted upon the
minds of the members by consistent usage in Mormon literature. Mormons have defined priesthood as
the sum of all divine authority and power, and they
believe that a small portion of that power is given to
each man as his "power of attorney," as it were, to
act in God's behalf. In doing so, he is said to "draw
upon the principle of the priesthood" and to "grow
in the principle of the priesthood" as well.

For Mormons and Catholics then, as McMurrin
points out, priesthood is regarded as a "real universal entity that does not have its reality grounded in
particular priests. Rather they are priests by virtue of
possession of the priesthood."[17] And this is what is
meant when Turner, in *Woman and the Priesthood*, re-
sponds to the question of why women can't hold the
priesthood by saying, "The answer lies in the character of the priesthood itself."[18] For women to gain
access to priesthood which is considered a universal,
and a male universal at that, would be a formidable
task indeed. To understand this problem is to recognize that there is a major difference in women being
able to say, "We want to be members of the
priesthood" and those who must say, "We want to
hold the priesthood."

In the Mormon Church then, where the view of
priesthood as a universal is combined with a belief

41

in modern revelation and an eternal marriage plan centered around the husband's priesthood, the prospects for women holding the priesthood themselves are extremely remote. While seldom analyzed in just that way, this is something Mormon women of today seem to sense. But on the subject, many of those I have interviewed also expressed a sense of something else that concerns them deeply. There is no question that the women of Mormondom have always been a comfortable distance from the actual priesthood, but apparently in early times they perceived they were closer to it than do women in the Church today. Historical accounts show that the Mormon sisters of the nineteenth century frequently received "gifts of the spirit" and participated in priesthood-like activities which the Church no longer finds acceptable for women. How can this inconsistency be explained? For one thing, in the formative stages of Mormon theology, it was not uncommon for the policies set forth to be revised or rescinded before the doctrine became stabilized. Additionally, it easily can be demonstrated that interpretations of different leaders over the years, in their subtle changes in emphasis, have continued to alter Mormon doctrine regarding spiritual activities of women.

With the purpose of justifying and glorifying the roles of women as outlined in Mormon doctrine, Turner prints selections from the writings and speeches of various church leaders which inadvertently illustrate these inconsistencies. Beginning with Joseph Smith, he relates a lecture the Prophet gave to the Mormon sisters in which he told them that by leading virtuous lives and keeping the commandments, they would "come into possession of the privileges, blessings, and gifts of the Priesthood, such as healing the sick and casting out devils."[19] Eliza R. Snow recorded a synopsis of the Prophet's remarks, and if she interpreted them correctly, women had no reason to believe their activities were restricted in those areas. She wrote: ". . .these signs, such as healing the sick, casting out devils, etc. should follow all that believe, whether male or female."[20]

Always with an eye for practicality, Brigham Young confirmed the teachings of Joseph Smith, phrasing it this way:

It is the privilege of a mother to have faith and to administer to her child; this she can do herself, as well as sending for the elders to have the benefit of their faith.[21]

With the elders involved in the important work of "building the kingdom," Brigham Young and his group of counselors regularly encouraged women to be self-sufficient. Realizing that success for the Saints depended upon maintaining a maximum cooperative effort, the males diplomatically bolstered the females' spirits along the way. In 1852, Elder Ezra Taft Benson, ancestor of the current Mormon authority, told the women, "The priests in Christendom warn their flocks not to believe in 'Mormonism'; and yet you sisters have the power to heal the sick by laying on hands, which they cannot do."[22]

Reinforced by their leaders, these dedicated pioneer women of early Mormonism were confident of their important position in the practical affairs of the community, and they enjoyed a veritable heyday in carrying out the spiritual affairs of the Church as well. Recorded in many diaries of the period are incidents of women "speaking in tongues," administering to the sick, washing and anointing, and standing in the priesthood circles when their babies were blessed (named). Utah writer Juanita Brooks recalls the story of a Mormon midwife called Grandma Mariah who lived in the area of St. George, Utah. So indispensable was her contribution, said Mrs. Brooks, that "they actually set her apart in the name of the priesthood."[23]

It is fascinating to discover that during this period of elevated status the Mormon sisters occasionally wrote as if equal power for women were a live question. Some of the active participants, particularly Eliza Snow, suggested that although they didn't have the right to reign at that time, they anticipated acquiring the power of reigning in some great eternal scheme of things.[24] It has been noted that Eliza Snow was the wife of Joseph Smith and later Brigham Young. But Eliza never became a mother, and as a result of this disappointment, she directed her considerable energies and talents to the affairs of the Church. While operatively Mormon women through the years have carried enough responsibility in their homes to make Mormondom seem like a matriarchy, Eliza Snow came closer to the actual leadership of the Church than any other woman in its history. It is not surprising under the circumstances that this capable and independent woman would come to regard women's leadership as logical. In fact, her opinions on church matters, which she rendered quite freely, occasionally conflicted with those of Brother Brigham and had to be countered by him.

Also a talented poet, Eliza Snow wrote the words to a hymn entitled "Oh My Father," describing a vision she had received of a Mother in Heaven as well as a Father. While this hymn was accepted by Mormon president Wilford Woodruff and others as a revelation, according to Mormon doctrine women can have revelations for themselves but not for the Church. As Turner explains, "Claims of females, such as the Virgin Mary appearing from heaven with messages for a church or for the world, are false."[25] Insisting that the voice of the priesthood is a male voice, he assures us that nowhere in all scripture is there record of any female being heard speaking on behalf of God, because "the Lord does not send women to do the work of men."

Regardless of impressions the women received from early Church leaders, healing the sick today is also considered the work of men. "It must be emphasized," Turner writes, "that the Priesthood presides. . . .It is only in the absence of the Priesthood that women are justified in independently exercising their own faith in seeking a healing blessing from the Lord."[26] And if, under those circumstances, women are unsure of their boundaries, he makes it clear that such ministrations are properly confined to children and other women "because only the Priesthood is authorized to bless all." Can it be concluded then that, in the absence of another priesthood member, a sick husband or a mature son would be required to go without a blessing rather than receive one from a woman?

While the restrictive attitudes expressed by Turner represent the views of the current Church authorities, this marked change, including doctrinal alterations on the subject, occurred in 1914 under Church President Joseph F. Smith. Perhaps women had become by then over-zealous in the use of their "gifts of the spirit," because the chief concern, unlike that of Brigham Young's day, was to curtail their spiritual activities. In 1921, Charles W. Penrose admitted there are occasions when perhaps it would be wise for a woman to lay her hands upon a child or another woman, granting that at times in the past this had been the case, but he continued with this admonition:

. . . that is all right, so far as it goes, but when women go around and declare that they have been set apart to administer to the sick and take the place that is given to the Elders by revelation, that is an assumption of authority and contrary to scripture.[27]

Such re-assertion of male authority finds a parallel in the early Christian Church. Sheila Collins in her book *A Different Heaven and Earth* points out that during Jesus' time and for a period shortly thereafter many women were as active as men in "spreading the Good News." Priscilla and her husband, Aquila, were described as "fellow workers in the Christ Jesus" (Romans 16:3) and Phoebe, whom Paul mentions in Romans 16:1, was believed to be a minister. According to Collins, Paul's well-known admonition to women to keep silent in the churches (1 Corinthians 14:34–35) was an indication that women were "becoming quite uppity, even to the point of prophesying and interpreting Scripture." She conjectures that there was probably a strong charismatic cast to their participation, as women have always seemed to gravitate toward this religious modality. Many New Testament scholars believe that the above doctrine and other glaring examples of anti-woman bias in the Epistles have wrongly been attributed to Paul, but may be the work of a later editor who added this gloss to the text at a time when the woman's role in the Church was becoming problematical. They are thought to have been written in the post-apostolic period in reaction to the freedom for women which Jesus endorsed. Collins notes that throughout Judeo-Christian history, whenever untrammeled freedom for women began to develop, it was poorly tolerated by males and followed with a stringent policy regarding women's roles.[28]

Some of the modern-day Mormon women who are acquainted with their history reflected wistfully upon that "golden age for women in Mormondom," though admittedly they didn't yearn for the hardships that went along with their spiritual independence and power. "But what satisfaction they must have felt in invoking their own faith in administering to the sick," commented one of the envious ones, "and how meaningful it must have been for a mother to join with the priesthood in naming her baby,"[29] a privilege she noted is no longer offered to women though occasionally a non-Mormon male such as a grandfather or special friend is included.

The obvious fact that Mormon women have lost the spiritual privileges they once enjoyed is not denied by Church leaders. Without apology, Turner offers what would be considered by them, no doubt, a reasonable explanation for this state of affairs:

While most women of today have ready access to the ministrations of the Priesthood, their pioneer sisters were often left to manage for themselves while their men-folk were away, sometimes for months and years. Consequently, those women relied upon the gifts of the spirit—especially healing—in caring for their families.

This is doubtless one reason why these gifts were, comparatively speaking, so common among them [30]

Mormon wives and mothers are advised, however, that the Saints in these last days will need all the divine assistance they can get, and therefore, they should continue to "magnify their spiritual potential." Observing that no one can say with certainty what the future will bring, Turner tells women of the Church that it is not impossible that some of them may yet, like their pioneer counterparts, be called upon to "round up their shoulders and carry some of the burdens normally borne by their fathers and husbands."[31] Like understudies in a play, Mormon women of the now established "kingdom of Zion" are directed to remain on standby, sufficiently prepared to rise into action in the event their spiritual contributions should be needed.

Although open criticism of the Church leadership is uncommon, my taped interviews for this book clearly indicate a growing awareness of the loss of status women have experienced as a result of these alterations. Claiming no disloyalty to the Prophets, one member suggested that "the Church doesn't always make refined or accurate distinctions between decisions that are God-inspired and those that are man-made and culturally determined."[32]

That Mormon women acknowledge that the priesthood is not within their reach should not imply that all of them are content with the arrangement. Portrayed by the Church as a burden as well as a privilege, the priesthood is not supposed to be an indication of power and superiority, but many of the sisters hastened to mention that priesthood power is misused frequently in the home, in the Church, and in the affairs of Mormon communities as well.

For some women the projected eternal paradise might be comfortable and appealing, but others who were interviewed recognize that even it does not promise equality. If men and women were indeed on equal footing, why would it be necessary for Church spokesmen to warn the woman that she should not envy her husband's position any more than he should envy the positions of his leaders? In fact, Turner goes so far as to say, "It is perhaps a greater sin for a woman to covet a man's priesthood than it would be for her to covet anything else,"[33] which feminist philosophers would quickly recognize as a device used by the patriarchy to maintain control of their system.

Without question, the Mormon patriarchy has created one of the most effective, well-protected systems of all religious organizations against infiltration by women. Nevertheless a small number of articulate critics insist that, as one woman expressed it, "the theological status of Latter-day Saint women has never been definitively set forth in this century, and the seeds sown by the heroines of the nineteenth century have never come to fruition."[34] At the risk of being labeled sinners, several of my interviewees confided that they do indeed covet priesthood for women. Viewing it as ultimately essential for the success of the culture, a few raised the interesting point that, in spite of the case against them, there is actually nothing that would preclude the possibility of gaining the priesthood through continuous revelation. "It is just that we are so culturally conditioned to think that it is out of the realm of the possible that no one wants to talk about it as a legitimate thing,"[35] says one of the hopefuls. Citing the abandoning of polygamy as an example of a major doctrinal alteration resulting from social pressure, one irrepressible optimist I talked with said, "Perhaps it's not as outrageous as it sounds."

Certainly nothing would have been considered too outrageous for the Mormons in the early days, according to journalist Tom Wolfe. In an article entitled "The Me Decade" in *New York Magazine*, Wolfe described the Mormon movement as the most famous of the many religious sects of the nineteenth-century "great awakening." Of the Mormons, he wrote, "This bunch was regarded as wilder, crazier, more obscene, more of a threat, than the entire lot of hippie communes of the 1960s put together." However, Wolfe went on to define a sect as a religion with no political power, and added that "once the Mormons settled, built, and ruled Utah, Mormonism became a religion sure enough . . . and eventually wound down to the slow, firm beat of respectability."[36]

Sterling M. McMurrin, considerably less flamboyant in style, made an assessment similar to that of Wolfe. Noting that Mormon theology is still young and unsophisticated with a structure that has yet to achieve internal consistency, McMurrin observes that "Yesterday it was vigorous, prophetic, and creative; today it is timid and academic and prefers scholastic rationalization to the adventure of ideas."[37] If the Mormons should happen to return to their former style, they might be well advised to explore new ideas concerning women's roles in the Church as a top priority. Though still representing only a minority, dissatisfaction with current policies comes from some of Mormonism's best educated and most caring members, including the woman who said, "If I have to think that priesthood for men is immutable and unchangeable as a sure God-given absolute—if that is true, I have a problem. If that is not true, I don't have a problem ultimately theologically, but I have a lot of problems institutionally now."[38]

Church leaders continue to reassure the world that Mormon women are the most fortunate of all women, but in fact an intense interest in problems related to feminism and the Mormon Church has developed throughout Mormondom. It has become the subject upon which Utah's increasing number of college and university women's conferences are focused. If all is truly well in Zion with regard to women, what forces are at work in the many over-crowded, emotionally-charged discussion sessions that are taking place? Is fear behind the tension and is guilt behind the tears? Is it something more than simple rationalization that allows a Mormon panelist to boast, "Yes, Virginia, there are Mormons who are feminists," without ever addressing the major feminist issues of leadership and power? Or is such a phenomenon in today's women's movement merely the result of "kinky thinking," as one feminist leader prefers to call it?

With its history of regulating women's spiritual participation in the Church as well as the practical affairs of their lives, the Mormon patriarchy has made its basic difference with feminism clear. It is not so important what decisions are being made as who is making the decisions.

But I want you to understand that the head of every man is Christ, the head of a woman is her husband, and the head of Christ is God.

1 Corinthians 11:3

3

MORMONS AND THE WORK ETHIC

Rooted in Mormon doctrine is an interesting philosophy regarding achievement that undoubtedly accounts for the impressive growth and economic success of the Latter-day Saint Church. On the other hand, the work traditions of the culture have been a source of some complex problems for some individuals, especially Latter-day Saint women. If their unique relationship to the priesthood sets Mormon women apart from their sisters throughout the world, the attitudes concerning work that have been

54

planted in their heads are equally distinctive. In continuing to explore the dynamics of the Mormon woman then, this chapter will discuss the features of Mormon doctrine that have shaped the work patterns of the culture, and the chapter following will discuss features of the work patterns that have shaped the Mormon woman.

The beehive was selected as the state symbol for Mormon Utah. No symbol could have been more appropriate for the flourishing Mormon kingdom and the general industriousness of the Mormon people. From the cradle, members of this productive society, male and female, are programmed to be achievers. So involved with activity are the Mormons that "work" certainly must be among the first words uttered by their infant members.

It is often assumed by non-Mormons that the strong work ethic of the Mormon culture is simply an intense expression of the Protestant work ethic, but it is something more. Though they both stem from the same philosophy about aggressive participation in the world being essential in life, the unusual Mormon view of human beings and their possibilities provides an added dimension.

The productive Mormon culture frequently has been compared to the achievement-oriented Jewish culture. The comparison has some validity. Because Mormons believe they are descendants of Israel chosen to re-establish a modern Zion on earth, they feel a strong identification with the ancient Hebrews

55

and have revived some of their customs. The difference in Jewish and Mormon attitudes toward achievement was described with humor recently by a Utah rabbi. "In the Mormon culture work is valued, any work. In the Jewish culture you only get credit if you succeed." The American Jewish people traitionally have shown a preference for excellence in scholarly pursuits. Mormons agree, but they also put a high value on work with the hands.

Cultural stereotypes are often misleading and generalizations can be dangerous—the material from which ethnic jokes are made—but they frequently contain a thread of truth that runs to the philosophical foundations of the culture. The Mormons can fairly be stereotyped as workers, and they have taken considerable pride in maintaining that image since it was established by the persevering Saints of the nineteenth century. A remarkable success story, the Mormon pioneer experience was not merely a demonstration of the courage and determination required of pioneers for survival. Beyond survival, the early Mormons were driven to accomplish the extraordinary by the work ethic which can be traced directly to their doctrine.

A variety of theological ideas were incorporated in the revealed doctrine of Joseph Smith. Only a few are actually exclusive to Mormonism, but in combination they have created the religion that is uniquely Mormon. Inherent in its doctrinal components is a theological formula for a productive society, motivat-

56

ing believers to function in such a distinctive manner that they have constituted an American subculture.

While Mormons are Christians, they depart radically from traditional Christianity by denying the doctrine of original sin and hence the doctrine of salvation by grace only. Although they accept the biblical account of Adam's fall quite literally, Mormons don't believe his fall rendered humans sinful by nature, unworthy, or without power to merit salvation. On the contrary, Mormonism interprets Adam's fall as a positive and essential event, entirely in keeping with God's will, which allowed human beings to gain knowledge of good and evil, the capacity for both, and most important, the full moral freedom to choose between them. According to Mormon doctrine it is this gift of moral freedom, called *free agency*, that gives men and women the capacity to live a life of moral endeavor and makes possible the development of genuine morality in the world.

In contrast to the teachings of Saint Augustine or Martin Luther, which were aimed at denigrating humankind, emphasizing its sinfulness and limitations, the teachings of Mormonism stress human freedom, human possibilities, and the natural disposition of human beings toward righteousness. With the free agency to choose righteousness over evil throughout their lives, Mormons believe they have the opportunity, in fact, the responsibility to earn their eternal salvation. The Latter-day Saints are not people who humbly rely upon God's merciful gift of grace to propel them to righteous deeds. The old adage "The Lord helps those who help themselves" is taken literally in Mormon country.

Their belief that they can merit salvation is not to imply that the Mormons have totally abandoned the doctrine of grace. It simply works in the opposite way from that of other Christian faiths. A common Christian tradition is that God's gift of grace releases the soul from sin, thereby making good works possible, that is, good works follow the gift of grace. For Mormons, God's grace is the gift of freedom to merit salvation through good works.

It easily could be assumed that such a doctrine would eliminate the necessity of the atonement of Jesus Christ for human salvation, which is not the case. Mormon theology allows that as a result of the fall man and woman were temporarily "banished from the garden" and given mortal life as a probationary period, as it were, to demonstrate their moral progress. Therefore, as McMurrin explains in *Theological Foundations of the Mormon Religion*, the Mormons believe that "by the grace of God through Christ it is made possible for man, who is by nature neither corrupt nor depraved, to merit salvation by free obedience to law."[1]

The nature of the salvation that can be earned in the Mormon eternal world, as previously noted, is specifically defined by doctrine. When Mormons are told of how the Lord will compensate each one according to his or her works, the greater the righteousness, the greater the rewards, they visualize those rewards in terms of degrees of glory. Occupying both time and space, the eternal world of the Mormons is divided into three such glories: the telestial which is the lowest, the terrestrial which is the middle, and the Celestial Kingdom, the highest glory available. As explained in Chapter 2, in attaining this highest of glories Mormons believe that as exalted spirits they shall dwell with God for eternity and will do so with the members of their earthly families. Given full understanding of what is required by the Mormon religion to qualify for the Celestial Kingdom, and aided by the concept of free agency, every Latter-day Saint can aspire to such a goal.

This remarkable life-affirming doctrine was introduced by Joseph Smith in nineteenth-century America when American society was caught up in the spirit of freedom and optimism about human possibilities and was rejecting the more negative and confining implications of traditional Puritanism. In such an atmosphere, this unusual religious innovation readily acquired a following. However, in discussing the theological foundations of Mormonism, McMurrin notes that some of these ideas which seemed so unusual did not originate with the Mormons. He points out that a similar doctrine regarding original sin was introduced in the first part of the fifth century by a British monk named Pelagius but in a less receptive environment. Apparently discouraged by man's dreary predicament, said to have resulted from Adam's fall, Pelagius suggested, among other things, that Adam's fall injured himself and nobody else and that there were men without sin before Christ's coming. A cheerful voice in the wilderness, Pelagius argued in those early days for man's salvation by merit. But Pelagius' ideas were promptly condemned by prominent theologians of the day, and for his creative contribution Pelagius was excommunicated by Pope Innocent I.

Of course, among absolutists Pelagius' radical notion that man was worthy enough to merit salvation, which challenged the omnipotence of God, was considered presumptuous if not outrageous. But Mormonism has had little difficulty with that problem because, in a second fundamental difference from established Christianity, Mormon theology denies the absoluteness of God. Instead of accepting the idea that God created the world *ex nihilo,* the Mormons were taught by their prophet that elements, including individual spirits or "intelligences," are eternal. Thus, "Man was also in the beginning with God."[2] Mormons believe that because human spirits are uncreated, having no beginning and no end, they are not altogether contingent upon God for existence; and, because the Mormon God is "a being among the beings rather than *being* as such, He is therefore finite rather than absolute."[3]

While the Mormon view of God as a man is not unusual in Christianity, their conception of God as related to the world and conditioned by it is unorthodox indeed. Subject to what the Saints call *eternal progression* Himself, this Mormon God has been involved in the struggle to overcome evil, and only through His own diligence in obeying eternal laws did He achieve mastery over the elements and reach His present state of perfection. The Mormon God is a self-made deity, as it were.

Having set such a fine example, formidable as it is, the God of the Mormons is perceived as a loving father who labors with humankind, guiding His sons and daughters to pattern their lives after Him. "Be ye therefore perfect, even as your Father which is in heaven is perfect," the Saints are counseled. While Mormons don't actually expect to equal the perfection of God, they believe, nevertheless, that a certain amount of perfection is within the reach of the devout. In fact, so great are the expectations of members of the Mormon faith, as we have already seen, that they believe each individual can achieve a degree of Godhood by unceasing effort in obeying commandments. As God is a deified man, so is each Mormon person a potential God or Goddess according to Mormon doctrine. Among organized religions of the world it would be difficult to find a comparable opportunity. Of course, in many religions this non-absolutistic, polytheistic doctrine would render the Mormons guilty of the traditional sin of pride, the first of the seven deadly sins.

With such a positive view of human potential, Mormonism might be considered the epitome of religious liberalism if it weren't for the fundamentalist features of the doctrine. Mormons still believe that in the final judgment, the sons of perdition shall be cast out and sentenced to eternal punishment. However, the sons of perdition in this case are mainly apostate Mormons. And a very real concern for the Mormon faithful is a powerful and deceitful Satan, a devil whose influence is so threatening that in the tug of war between good and evil he has managed to win over one-third of the spirits. Nevertheless, in the Mormon plan, it is clearly the individual's own decision whether he will follow the devil or invest his efforts in the future exalted life. As Brigham Young warned his people, "Here is the platform, and if men are not saved, it is their own fault."[4]

Certainly, divergence from traditional Christianity on these major religious issues has placed Mormonism in a category all its own. Some of the original liberal views of the Mormon Church regarding human potential are often disregarded by the current Mormon leadership. In recent decades Mormon leaders have been moving toward an increasingly traditional and conservative religious position, describing human beings in more negative terms. For example, in 1976 President Spencer Kimball made reference to "puny, irresponsible, presumptuous man who dares to change the laws of God."[5] But regardless of the conservative trend, the positive philosophy rooted in Joseph Smith's revelations gave vitality to the Mormon movement and continues to have a profound effect upon the behavior of the membership as a motivating force. It is the theological framework of the Church and the basis of the religious conditioning of its members.

Early in life impressionable Mormon children learn that they must obey the commandments if they want to live with their Father in Heaven, and that each is a special child of God who has inner God-like qualities which must be cultivated. It isn't long before they understand the familiar Mormon phrases "magnify your calling" and "develop your potential." After baptism at the age of eight, which in the Mormon Church is not for release from original sin, but for forgiveness of the actual accumulated sins of the individual, young Mormons are held accountable for their actions. At that point, with God as a model, they begin their lifelong climb on the ladder that extends from the earth to the Celestial Kingdom of God, reaching each new rung on the ladder through obedience, diligence, and self-improvement.

Keeping close tabs on all the members, the Church acknowledges achievement along the way by graduating them from one level to another in its various organizations. However, advancement in the Mormon Church might be compared to an athletic contest in which boys enjoy a significant advantage. Seeming to skip rungs on the ladder, law-abiding young males progress so rapidly that by the time they reach the age of twelve they are given the priesthood, while wholesome LDS maidens at the same age are given only encouragement. In any case, they all become involved in the essential process of *eternal progression*, a process that is expected to remain uppermost in the minds of the faithful.

Because males and females at the early age of twelve begin traveling separate paths toward the Celestial Kingdom, there are several important differences in their progression patterns. Following the life of a devout Mormon male first, it is customary for him to mark the passage from youth to manhood by a two-year mission for the Church. Frequently, wayward youths who have been misusing their free agency are also sent off on missions for the purpose of reconditioning. Operating the largest missionary program in the world, the Mormon Church currently maintains approximately twenty-five thousand missionaries each year, proselyting on every continent and in almost every country.

His mission credit established, the adult LDS male is then expected to marry, to begin producing children, and to continue participating actively in church affairs. Those who demonstrate the greatest commitment to the Church and devotion to its principles become eligible to serve as church leaders. Such positions not only carry considerable social status in Mormon communities, but also command respect that suggests a head start in the deification process. A qualified male can be chosen by men in higher positions to serve in the bishopric of his neighborhood church or ward, and can progress to the presidency of the stake, a division composed of several wards. The most righteous and effective leaders then advance in the authoritarian hierarchy to the general leadership of the Church. And as they advance in the hierarchy, they gain in authority until, upon reaching the Council of Twelve, they are labeled, in fact, *General Authorities.* Operating on the seniority system, the top-ranking member of the Council becomes President of the Church upon the death of his predecessor, and upon assuming that office, he achieves the status of "prophet, seer, and revelator." Then, serving as a liaison between man and God, the Mormon Church President is regarded by many as a man who has earned at least partial deification while still on earth, the ultimate in earthly eternal progression.

Unlike the majority of faiths which require scholarly preparation for the clergy, the Mormon Church provides its leaders with lifelong experience and on-the-job training. Thus, in the Mormon lay clergy system, the leadership can be composed of devout men with a variety of backgrounds. It is a curious fact, however, that those in charge of the Church have been predominantly successful businessmen whose family names have appeared repeatedly throughout Mormon history. Whether spirits borne into prominent Mormon families are endowed more abundantly with righteousness or their rise in the hierarchy is of a political nature as some critics suggest, the eternal progression of well-named Mormon spirits is noticeably accelerated. The Mormon aristocracy is recognized as a prevailing force in the system and derives its status more from a heritage of church leadership than from accumulated wealth.

While the men have been busy advancing through various authoritarian positions in the church organization, what prescribed course have the women been following? Again, success is measured according to church service and adherence to Mormon principles. And, with marriage and motherhood as requirements for eternal progression, sometimes an additional barometer for determining a woman's righteousness is in the number of children she produces. Her path does not direct her to the leadership of the Church, but as a reward for a fine performance as a church worker, she can be appointed by male leaders to head church auxiliary organizations. Such positions, including the coveted presidency of the Relief Society, cannot begin to yield for women the status their male counterparts enjoy. Nevertheless, the active Latter-day Saint woman is revered in her community and her accomplishments within the institution demonstrate that she is making headway toward the eternal goal.

In the design of the Mormon system of eternal progression, it is clear that a woman, lagging behind since childhood, is not really meant to become equal to a man any more than a man is expected to become equal to God, no matter how remarkable his progression. But, in spite of that, women of the Church are reminded regularly by authorities that "the gospel elevates women like nothing else." To emphasize an extremely significant point that was discussed earlier, it is because women are offered an opportunity to earn exaltation as goddesses in the Celestial Kingdom that Mormon spokesmen feel justified in claiming that their women have the most elevated position, the greatest freedom, and the greatest opportunities of all women everywhere—in the face of worldly evidence to the contrary. To those unfamiliar with their doctrine, Mormon leaders attempting to explain this paradox seem to be speaking in "Mormon tongues," their vision of a cosmic utopia being far beyond the comprehension of secular critics.

Nevertheless, as far as the work ethic is concerned, the Mormon Church has managed to instill a strong sense of personal worth in both males and females, albeit relative, and has provided each with some highly attractive goals. Thus, its members have been naturally motivated toward increased righteousness and good works. But the traditional good works of religion have not been equated necessarily with the kind of industriousness regularly seen in Mormon communities. Religious good works traditionally include overt acts of charity and kindness, and they involve such elusive virtues as faith, humility, honesty, and love. After the Reformation, the Protestant philosophy encouraged industriousness, stressing the holiness in man's role in daily life, and that brought about a surge of activity among Christians. But even the Reformation cannot account for the extraordinary range of activities performed by the Mormons in the name of religion. Only by closely examining the nature of Mormon "good works" and what obeying the commandments entails for men and women of the society can the Mormon work ethic and the extent of its influence be understood.

To begin with, the Mormon religion assumed a practical, this-worldly character as a reflection of its unusual conception of deity. Though the eternal world is clearly the ultimate concern, it was determined early that the activities of the Saints would focus on the here and now when Joseph Smith's revelations named them as a people *chosen* to establish God's kingdom on this continent, a literal, material kingdom. As previously noted, it was after several abortive attempts to build the kingdom elsewhere in the United States that Utah was designated as the proper place, and the kingdom that was to succeed was launched by Brigham Young.

Organized and assigned a variety of necessary tasks by their innovative leader, the early kingdom builders performed their tasks with religious fervor, demonstrating the practical approach to religion and the practice of daily faith that has continued to characterize the Mormons through the years. In a typical Mormon work-promoting message, Brigham Young explained to the pioneers:

The Lord has promised to provide for His Saints, to feed

and clothe them, but He expects them to plough and to plant, sow and reap, and prepare their bread from the increase of the soil.[6]

In addition to agricultural endeavors, the initial building of the kingdom meant the cutting of forests, the watering of the desert, and the building of dams and houses.

Today the Saints have the task of maintaining a prosperous and growing kingdom, a job that requires extensive effort simply in the operation of its institutions and includes expansion and development of a variety of large-scale agricultural and commercial enterprises. From pioneer times to the present day, this work of the kingdom has been accepted by the Mormons as their primary vocation—the work that will lead to eternal salvation.

From the beginning the Saints have been made to understand that unceasing effort must go into the building of the kingdom rather than mere token contributions. "We are required to perform works of righteousness all the day long," counseled Brigham Young's assistant, Jedediah M. Grant. "Brothers, you are required to be very diligent," he said. Reprimanding those who seemed inclined toward laziness, Brother Grant continued:

Some think that they have already labored enough to obtain heaven. Many of those who have come with hand carts think they have done wonders. Therefore, they want every hat hoisted in deference to them and every meal bag gratuitously opened, and they want everybody to feed, clothe and lodge them, and find them everything they need just because they have dragged a hand cart across the plains.[7]

He assured the weary pioneers that they deserved credit for what they had done, "but I make this observation that you may know that you have not yet got into the harbor of eternal life."

While Mormon doctrine and its basic religious obligations are set forth in the official church books, *The Book of Mormon, The Doctrine and Covenants,* and *The Pearl of Great Price,* Mormons, having established an hierarchal form of government, have always looked to their current leaders for guidance in affairs of the kingdom. And religious leaders in charge of kingdom development are by definition pragmatic leaders. Of necessity, they show unusual concern for the temporal affairs of their members, often viewing secular progress as synonymous with spiritual progress. The General Authorities have the responsibility of adapting to the changing needs of the kingdom and of protecting its interests politically, materially, and socially, so an interesting variety of additional "good works" for Mormons regularly are defined from the pulpit.

Thus, since the days of Brigham Young, the Saints have gathered at the semiannual Church conferences on Temple Square in Salt Lake City to receive instructions from their Prophet and his counselors. And while the delivery of the messages today is sometimes bland compared with that of Brother Brigham, the content still has a distinctive Mormon flavor, frequently described as "folksy." The presentations run the gamut from lofty, inspirational words to practical, homely advice. Viewed on world-wide television by satellite, a 1976 conference session, for example, featured typical Christian sermons on love, faith, and prayer and speeches in praise of Mormonism. There were warnings against the moral decadence stemming from our permissive society, including condemnation of abortion and sterilization, improper use of sex (homosexuality and "fondling of bodies"), divorce, drugs, and pornography, all categorized as moral issues and therefore legitimate concerns of the church. At the same time, however, leaders counseled members to mend broken fences, to clean up their homes and farms, and to clear weedy ditch banks, and they noted that some had been neglecting the important duty of storing a year's supply of food. Instructed to plant fruit trees and gardens in their back yards, the Saints also were cautioned that if they didn't fill their fruit bottles they might regret it. Exhorting his people to be obedient, to attend meetings, and to work hard every day, President Kimball concluded the conference with a reminder that Mormons should "heed conference messages because we haven't been fooling."[8] The atmosphere of a Latter-day Saints conference is charged with Mormon industrious spirit and traditionally is a call to action. Mormonism has been

71

recognized from the start as an active rather than a contemplative religion. As spoken plainly by Brigham Young, "More testimonies are obtained on the feet than on the knees."[9]

The majority of the faithful are prepared, in fact, to heed conference messages as directed. Because they are all in this undertaking together, the Mormons, wherever they are, have developed a sense of unity and cohesiveness that is rare in religious organizations. And their cooperative spirit is reinforced by the sense of specialness or separateness instilled in them by virtue of being chosen. "We are the Saints of God," they are reminded, "not ordinary people." While this attitude has the discriminatory effect of rendering all others "unchosen" and continues to feed the fires of Mormon/non-Mormon controversy, it has been the power behind Mormonism.

The church operation thrives upon a massive volunteer effort in which every family and individual member is expected to contribute like a cog in the wheel. With a job for everyone and several for some, church work for the Latter-day Saints easily can become a full-time commitment. Of course, what is good for the kingdom is good for the individual. Advancing socially as well as spiritually in proportion to his or her contribution, the individual enjoys personal gains from efforts directed toward group goals.

The Utah rabbi was correct in his assessment that any productive work is valued in the Mormon culture It takes all kinds of work to build a kingdom, and to use a proverbial Mormon expression, "There is no excellence without labor." In their group endeavor, the Mormons have learned that "every earthly task, however apparently humble, however apparently remote from fundamental principles, has a spiritual counterpart." Leaders have stressed to the workers that "all such tasks are proper, dignified, and necessary parts of the Great Plan, and will lead man along the path of eternal progression."[10]

It has been apparent that Mormons have placed unusual emphasis on commitment to the group, but Mormonism has not overlooked the fact that the group is only as strong as its individual members. It must be remembered that the development of individual potential is also a commandment of the religion, and the goal of perfection toward which each Saint is progressing cannot be accomplished simply through devoted service to the Church and reaching an elevated spiritual state. It must encompass the acquiring of knowledge and the development of skills and talents as well as every aspect of the personality. So important is the pursuit of knowledge in the Saints' plan of eternal progression, in fact, that it is said to be impossible to be saved in ignorance. "The glory of God is intelligence,"[11] according to Mormon doctrine, and the knowledge attained in this life is believed to rise with the individual into the eternal world. With God's transcendence conceived as the ultimate in self-improvement, the Mormons expect that "advancement in all areas hastens exaltation" for each individual member.

With total development of both the individual and the kingdom as religious priorities, it is easy to see how work has emerged as one of the important religious principles in Mormonism. "The principles of work are to be taught in the family, and children are not to be spared from work,"[12] the Church President reminded the members at a 1973 conference. To supplement the basic home training, the Mormon leadership provides practical, continuous instruction regarding the work principle, outlining methods for using time wisely and increasing efficiency. With their religion requiring unusual diligence in pursuing earthly goals as well as in following Christ's teachings, it might be said that Mormons, following their doctrine of salvation by merit, literally work their way to eternal salvation.

If an individual raised in the Mormon environment escapes the influence of the culture, it is not because of negligence on the part of the Church. Leaving nothing to chance, the Mormons have organized developmental programs and activities that involve family members throughout the week. Requiring a sizable expenditure of time and energy in their operation and administration, these "programs of the Lord" serve the dual purpose of training the membership and further binding them together in the process. If, for some, organized religion means worshipping together, for the Latter-day Saints it means worshipping, working, playing, and learning together.

In its all-consuming approach to the religious experience, the Mormon religion, unlike some others, emphasizes physical pleasures as well as spiritual well-being. Compatible with the positive Mormon philosophy of human potential, *The Book of Mormon* states, "Men are that they might have joy." The Mormons have become accustomed to organized recreation on a grand scale. In addition to providing pleasure, Mormon programmed recreation has created a forum for individual growth and the means whereby the values of the culture can be cemented. Through Church-sponsored sports as well as dancing and theatrical events, which are wholeheartedly endorsed by the Church, latent talents are discovered and cultivated. And with the multitude of group activities from the Mormon-operated Boy Scouts of America program to family church suppers, at which Mormon women excel, the qualities of leadership and self-expression are developed. While it is not mandatory for Mormons to play the games of the kingdom, there is the assumption that assisting with and participating in Mormon recreation will aid in eternal progression.

While focusing primarily upon religious indoctrination, the educational system within the Church is also highly structured. Lesson plans for various church and auxiliary organizations, including the

Mormon "Family Home Evening," are designed and coordinated in the central offices of the Church and distributed to Mormons around the world. They come complete with workbooks, visual aids, and cassette tapes and are promoted with bumper stickers bearing such messages as "Happiness is Family Home Evening." Uniformity is considered a desirable goal, and teachers are instructed to follow the church-approved plans carefully.

That education is highly prized in the culture is reflected in the high percentage of Utahns attending college, frequently the highest in the nation. Because of the cultural values toward achievement, Utah has shown outstanding productivity in many scholarly fields. Yet, the subject of Mormons and education presents one of the most striking paradoxes of the culture. The source of Mormon pride is the target of Gentile criticism. It is generally conceded by outsiders that the Saints "made the desert blossom as a rose," but roses notwithstanding, the Mormons often are accused of creating an intellectual desert with a climate that prohibits genuine mental development. The purpose of education for Mormons is to justify dogma, critics charge, and therefore "behind the Zion curtain" many feel the scope of education is, in fact, quite limited. Readily admitting that the Church views philosophical systems with considerable suspicion, the Mormon patriarchy often warns the members against accepting the wisdom of the world over the advice of Church leaders. "When our leaders speak," said one of the authorities, "the thinking has been done."[13] So while Mormons are deemed righteous in acquiring knowledge, they are restricted to the "right" knowledge and discouraged from questioning and exploring ideas. In fact, even on subjects other than religion, a kind of "group think" has evolved in Mormondom as a result of its uniform approach to education, which, according to observers of the system, does not readily accommodate original thoughts and divergent opinions. In primarily breeding doers instead of thinkers, the high-achieving Mormon culture could be evaluated as pro-education and anti-intellectual simultaneously.

With the General Authorities billed, as their name implies, as the chief educational source for the vast Mormon empire, education can move in some interesting directions. Cautioning the Saints to "beware the philosophies of men," these educators, though authorized to speak the words of God, are themselves mortal beings and subject to human error. When counseling members out of their wisdom, some cannot resist expressing personal opinions on a broad variety of issues. Showing a marked tendency toward ultra-conservative political philosophy, certain leaders, for instance, have enlisted the naturally adaptive Mormon theology to fortify their own views. Inadvertently distorting its meaning, they speak of the Mormon doctrine of free moral agency in connection with political freedoms they espouse, such as freedom from "big government," and suggest that *The Book of Mormon* be used as a weapon against the growing socialism in America. The indoctrination of members into right-wing political extremism has caused much uneasiness in and around the kingdom because a sizable liberal faction of the culture still considers it prudent to avoid combining political orientation with Church lessons. However, such are the hazards of education, Mormon style.

Of course, it is important to remember that the current Church authorities of conservative political persuasion did not plant the idea of economic self-sufficiency in the heads of the Mormons. The Saints' preoccupation with self-reliance, which is said to be so imperative that "salvation can be obtained by no other principle," has always included economic self-sufficiency as an important aspect. In fact, from the way in which Mormon theology and work have become intertwined, it is easy to see why economic self-sufficiency has been interpreted by many as the primary goal of education. In that context, it is not unreasonable for Mormons to have the notion that prospering in the world is an indication of spiritual growth.

Certainly, throughout Mormon history the making of money has not been considered demeaning or undesirable in any way. There is so much disdain for money mismanagement, in fact, that Church officials have included training members in the field of finance among their religious responsibilities. In a twelve-point program presented to the membership in 1971, the Church offered advice on such problems as budgeting, insurance, and investment programs. Latter-day Saint leaders repeatedly have admonished their people to "get out of debt and stay out," and in connection with the Idaho dam disaster of 1976, which affected a community of Mormons, President Kimball explained to the Associated Press, "We teach our people to provide for themselves, to earn their way, and not to receive a lot of doles."

Caring for their own needy, the Mormon Church rejects Federal welfare and instead operates an effective welfare system within the Church, complete with welfare farms and stores. But because the Church believes that it is important for people "to maintain self-respect in time of adversity," the recipients of Mormon welfare are expected to reciprocate in some way. "The Lord has directed His disciples to rely on their own work," they have been told.

In terms of free enterprise, Mormonism is American idealism converted to religion. If, with the passage of time, that idealism has diminished in America, it has been altered very little among the Mormons since Brigham Young preached it in the early days. That pioneer leader instructed the sisters of the Relief Society to visit the sick and helpless and needy to learn of their wants and needs, but he also said, "Relieving them requires something beyond present necessities. If giving encourages idleness, it

has a demoralizing tendency." Brigham agreed that
the women should go ahead helping the sick, but

if a person has strength to labor, it is far more charitable to
give employment, and so direct their energies that they
can earn what they need, and thus, realize the fruits of
their own labors.[14]

With an unusual work ethic rooted in an unusual
theology, the Mormons themselves are often viewed
as unusual in American society. On the other hand,
considering the nature of their philosophy of work,
Mormons could be thought of as super-Americans in
a kingdom that is the essence of American society.
The entire organizational network of the Latter-day
Saints is designed to perpetuate hard work and self-
sufficiency as basic requirements of the religion, and
the men and women of the culture have grown up
knowing that "the surest helping hand is at the end
of their own sleeve."

*Mormons can be said to enjoy a kind of
sweet-pea freedom. A human analogue to the
individual blossom of the sweet pea might be
seen in the young maiden freely going to Sab
bath school—her raiment clean and brightly
colored, her hair neatly waved, wind-blown
or ratted according to her tuste, the bloom on
her cheeks concealed by just the right amount
of drugstore luster, and the thoughts she will
think that day carried in a manual in her
hand. A perfect specimen of her kind.*

Waldemer P. Read

4

DOUBLE DOSE OF THE

DOUBLE MESSAGE

Unquestionably, the industrious Mormon Saints
have created an extraordinary *temporal* kingdom. To
what extent can their efforts in carrying out what
they believe to be "God's plan" be labeled successful? As one clear indicator of their success, the membership of the Mormon Church has grown at an astonishing rate, approaching the four million mark in
less than a century and a half. Noting their four
hundred per cent increase of the past thirty years,

President Spencer Kimball rejoiced, "Truly we are filling the earth."

When measured in terms of material growth, the progress of the Mormons is even more impressive. A 1976 Associated Press report named the Mormon Church the wealthiest religious organization in the nation, estimating that the Church, with the corporations it controls, has revenues of more than three million dollars a day. In fact, in total assets, the Latter-day Saint Church is ranked among the top fifty corporations in America. As President Kimball explained when questioned on the NBC "Today Show" about the economic pursuits of the Mormon kingdom, "It takes a great amount of money to build the growing Church of Jesus Christ of Latter-day Saints."

A set of values is reflected by the Mormon society, and most of the values are positive. Among them the high regard for the family stands out as a solid, stabilizing force. At a time when dissolution of the family is threatening the western world, it would be difficult to foresee its devaluation in the Mormon culture. And of course, by providing its people with clearly defined purpose and a sense of belonging, the kingdom would be considered successful by any sociological standards. In praising this outstanding Mormon heritage, one church leader pointed out that "you cannot have the fruits of Mormonism without the roots of Mormonism."

However, some of the fruits of Mormonism are bit-

ter fruits Several of the kingdom's shortcomings
have been suggested in preceding chapters. Additionally, there is one major flaw in the system which
in recent years has become increasingly apparent. It
would be difficult for Americans to view a work ethic
as anything but praiseworthy, but the way in which
the Mormon work ethic has been translated in terms
of women is at last provoking some justifiable criticism. In fact, in these days of women's awakening, it
is a problem that threatens to create havoc within the
Mormon organization.

It is important to remember that women as well as
men within the Mormon culture are conditioned to
be achievers, and in their diligence, many young
women demonstrate laudable talents and scholastic
aptitudes. It is entirely in accordance with cultural
expectations that such women pursue a college education, ideally at the Church-operated Brigham
Young University. But college is usually the end of
the line for their scholastic endeavors because, during that four-year period, societal goals for women
shift away from academics, and the certificate they
are expected to earn at college is the marriage certificate.

Is that so different from non-Mormon women?
Haven't females across the country complained
about the proverbial double message they receive, a
message that says, "We want you to achieve academ-
ically, but what we really want is for you to marry
and settle down"? For Mormon women the messages

are stronger and the dilemma is greater because pressure comes not only from family and society in general, but also directly from Mormon doctrine in the form of religious commandment. Simultaneously, Mormonism teaches its law of eternal progression, encouraging productivity and achievement as a primary religious duty, and its law of eternal marriage, designating marriage and parenthood as the primary religious duty. Thus, the devout Mormon woman is a woman with limited options for achievement, and this can lead to a frustrating predicament if she is motivated and talented.

While these religious laws always have existed side by side in Mormon doctrine, the contradiction therein has been intensified in recent decades by the outpouring of messages from the patriarchy, many of which have been designed to counter the steady flow of messages from feminists. In a speech entitled "Woman's Movement, Liberation or Deception?" in 1971, Mormon authority Elder Thomas Monson labeled the women of the movement "Pied Pipers of sin who have led women away from the divine rule of womanhood down the pathway of error." Monson assured the Mormon sisters that ". . . the truly happy woman is she who is filling the full measure of her creation by nobly bearing and raising a family of healthy children." In fact, he concluded that,

. . . so long as Mormon women cling to the simple ideal of home and joyous family life, so long as they feel the measure of their creation is homemaker, so long is the Church and nation safe.[1]

Responding to a question about women's roles in an interview with United Press International in January 1974, President Kimball confirmed this position of the Church. "Generally speaking," said the prophet, "women should remain in the home. To bear children and raise a family—that is their most sacred calling. Any other course may be disastrous." Thus, women responding to their "sacred calling" are liberally praised by the Church, but those who entertain thoughts of delaying marriage are warned not to be deceived by "doctrines of the devil."[2]

It is popular today for young married couples outside of the Mormon kingdom who haven't decided against raising a family to delay their families in order to pursue their separate career objectives. But for dutiful Latter-day Saints, such a decision could not be sanctioned, because delaying children also is considered "the work of the devil" by Mormon leaders. "Accept all the spirits (children) the Lord sees fit to send you," advises President Kimball, who also expresses his opposition to the practice of young women working to finance their husbands' education. "Let the children come," he counsels the young marrieds of Zion. "It will all work out."[3]

Unless assuming the additional task of head of the household causes undue financial stress, males have no problem fulfilling a family commitment while simultaneously advancing in their chosen fields, but the mechanics of combining a career and family are notoriously difficult for women; nevertheless, many courageous American women have accepted that challenge. But in spite of the Mormon respect for hard work, the present church leaders also are discouraging that alternative for Latter-day Saint women. Instead of receiving admiration for their ambitious undertaking, women with both families and careers are labeled selfish or materialistic.

A harsh critic of working mothers, Church official H. Burke Peterson charged in 1974 that women leave home to take jobs

... more for luxuries cloaked in the masquerade of necessity or a so-called opportunity for self-development of talents in the business world; a chance to get away from the mundane responsibilities of the home.

While obviously agreeing that home maintenance is mundane, Peterson pointed out that such reasons are all "Satanic substitutes for clear thinking, . . . counterfeit thoughts that subvert the responsibilities of motherhood."[4]

And comments from Mormon leader Ezra Taft Benson on this type of behavior have been equally forceful. "Let me warn the sisters in all seriousness," he admonishes,

... the mother who entrusts her child to the care of others

that she may do non-motherly work, whether for gold or fame or for civic service, should remember that a child left to himself bringeth his mother to shame.[5]

Not only do working mothers have a detrimental effect upon their children, according to Mormon authorities, they are repeatedly blamed for weakening the institution of marriage. Even with compelling financial needs, Latter-day Saint mothers are made to understand that "a child needs more of a mother than of money" and that their duty is to be "home by the hearthside." Of course, they are made to understand at the same time that accepting welfare is not in keeping with Mormon principles.

With their training from childhood reflecting this choice of emphasis by the patriarchy, the predicament of Mormon women should come as no surprise. Nevertheless, some of the college-educated Mormon mothers pointed out in my interviews that the Church policy of restricting women as homemakers seemed to be in direct conflict with the Church's stress on individual growth. Because some of these women have looked to history and have taken inspiration from their remarkable ancestors, they are well aware that the female role models from their Mormon heritage were recognized and praised by the Saints for their professional and vocational accomplishments as much, if not more than, for their homemaking skills. Some have noticed that it was only after the Mormon kingdom became reasonably secure economically that the leadership began emphasizing the traditional sex roles of the Bible.

Now, with the kingdom on its feet, church authorities can preach confidently that "men and women are assigned to the division of labor in the home and Church for which each is best suited by nature. The woman is the child bearer and rearer and homemaker," they say, "and the man is the provider." But that was a risky assumption when the kingdom was getting underway. It was much safer for Brigham Young and his men to encourage and direct women to do some of the providing, as explained in the following epistle:

Mothers in Israel, you are called upon to bring up your daughters to pursue some useful vocation for a sustenance, that when they shall become wives of the elders, who are frequently called upon missions, or to devote their time and attention to the things of the kingdom, they may be able to sustain themselves and their offspring.[6]

And sustain themselves they did. As we saw in Chapter 1, no doors were closed to pioneer Mormon women in regard to work. There was hardly a task or profession which ultimately did not require the participation of women, from building houses and running farms to the practicing of medicine and law. The developing of marketable skills for women then was an economic necessity.

If the above section of Brigham Young's epistle on the training of women is no longer relevant as the Church operates today, the second part of that epistle expressed another philosophy that has remained consistent in Mormonism through the years:

Teach them to sew, spin, weave, and knit, as well as to embroider, to cultivate vegetables as well as flowers, to milk, make butter and cheese, and work in the kitchen as well as in the parlor. Thus, will you and your daughters show yourselves approved, and prove helpmeets in very deed, not only in the domestic relations, but in building up the kingdom also.[7]

With their employment outside of the home curtailed, Mormon women still receive practical training in the home arts, and today they are characterized primarily by their expertise in homemaking skills.

As women's financial contributions diminished, they naturally lost some of their independence. And now, with the majority of the brethren able to support their wives financially, they occasionally can be heard idealizing motherhood and womanhood and speaking of women as delicate creatures who require special care. But in actuality, the typical Mormon woman, conditioned by her work-oriented culture, is still a relatively self-reliant and capable "woman who can do a good day's work." While the custom of catering to women might come to pass eventually, as far as work is concerned the fostering of dependency in women goes against Mormon tradition. Employing the doctrine of free agency, again in a somewhat questionable manner, Brigham Young established that idea from the beginning:

... The women come and say, "Really Brother John and Brother William, I thought you were going to make a heaven for me," and they get into trouble because a heaven is not made for them by the men, even though agency is upon women as well as men.[8]

The Mormon woman as a *worker*, then, remains a clearly established fact, but regarding the *use* of her energy, once again there has been inconsistency among the conveyers of God's wishes in the Mormon leadership. And here feminists should take note. The current authorities no doubt would justify their curtailment of women's activities outside the home for the same reason they have commanded women to cease exercising their gifts of the spirit. Because the kingdom has a sufficient number of men available for such jobs, women's contributions are no longer needed. However, if Mormon leaders can explain that Brigham Young's conception of the woman's sphere was appropriate only for his time, aren't patriarchal leaders themselves reinforcing that most important of feminist arguments against them? Certainly, if the attitudes of Brigham Young, a Mormon prophet, could be declared outdated in society today, it would be reasonable to assume that the philosophy of Paul and early theologians regarding women's

"God-given roles" are not immutable but could be dismissed as invalid on the same grounds.

Troubled and bewildered by the restrictive position of the patriarchy, this time as it pertains to women's work outside of the Church, some Mormon women whom I have interviewed express several concerns. They worry that in zealously pontificating that the woman's place is in the home, authorities are overlooking the reality that countless women must work for a living, thereby inflicting criticism and adding guilt to the already heavy burdens they carry.

The obvious conflict resulting from the Church's double message is verbalized again and again. While some women admit that for their many accomplishments much of the credit must go to the Church, they consider it a strange irony that, as one phrased it, "Church leaders think somehow women can take all that education and channel it down one narrow tube."[9] Another from the growing ranks of critics commented, "We've been educated to take part in this world, and we should be allowed to take it. Instead," she noted, "the Church wants women to go home, shut the door, and stay there."[10]

While partially true, this assessment of the Church's motives omits a very significant point regarding what the leaders actually have in mind for Mormon women today. If they are expected to go home and shut the door, they also are expected to burrow a tunnel to the nearest church. Having grown to enormous proportions, Mormonism today absolutely must rely upon its women to perpetuate the system. What the Church needs now from the sisters is not their economic assistance. The greatest services Mormon women can perform for the kingdom at this time are to operate its programs, to insure continuing family involvement, and to train young members in the Mormon way of life. And by shuttling back and forth between home and church, the women of Mormondom can strengthen the ties that will protect the kingdom against the threatening influences of the outside world.

Herein lies the crux of the problem and the source of extensive misunderstanding. Critics who say women are not valued in Mormon society are mistaken. The fact is, women's services to the Church are so valuable that the system cannot afford to have them running around pursuing their own interests. In taking an arbitrary stand on women's roles, it is not that Church authorities are opposed to women's rights per se; and with its unusual work ethic, the culture naturally would be proud of high-achieving women under different circumstances. But it must be remembered that the kingdom is a group operation, and groups are not accustomed to considering individual needs before group causes. For that reason, women who are involved totally with Church work, having the equivalent of a full-time job, are praised, if not "sainted," while other working women are warned against seeking "personal aggrandizement." Considering the women's movement's emphasis upon self-fulfillment, there is little wonder that the Mormon leadership has expressed its strong opposition.

Concerning the perplexing problem of highly educated Mormon women, Church leaders count such women as particular assets, assuming their education will be shared with fellow Latter-day Saints in the developmental programs of the Church. Because the purpose of education for women, as defined by the authorities, is to help them become better mothers, the patriarchs do not recognize that a problem exists. Instead, they actively encourage continuing education for women so that "they will be prepared to direct their children in proper paths." They proudly reassure the sisters that "the Church provides the opportunity for women to grow in their role."

That opportunity is to be found in the Relief Society, which is said to be designed to meet all women's needs, including education. Based on the principle of service, the Relief Society is "part of the Church plan for salvation" and therefore is deemed "vital to the welfare of every Latter-day Saint woman and family." Its stated purpose is to enlarge the scope of women's activities, but unfortunately some of its members express dismay because instead, the Relief Society currently reflects the preoccupation of the patriarchy with restricting women's activities. And the intellectual stimulation provided by the Relief Society fails to satisfy some of the more scholarly sisters, many of whom observe that education is offered only in so far as it relates to family preparedness and home skills. Nevertheless, in answer to critics who have questioned the intellectual growth of Mormon women as a group, the Church president rises to their defense: "Latter-day Saint women are among the best educated and trained in the world."[11]

Far from being a sinister lot plotting against their women, Mormon Church leaders are honorable, even altruistic, in designing an effective system to meet the needs of all their people. It is no doubt with utmost sincerity that Turner, in *Woman and the Priesthood*, poses the question on behalf of the Church, "How could any woman with understanding feel that her calling is beneath her?"[12] Yet, it is not within the scope of understanding of the Mormon patriarchy that a woman might feel that the calling to which he refers, while not necessarily "beneath her," is not her calling at all. And several University of Utah staff members have verified that many hours of the counseling day are spent in helping students resolve that conflict.

Wishing to adhere to church principles, but unwilling to abandon career goals, the determined ones forge ahead with both, with intentions to excel in all areas. Since the nineteenth century, in fact, Mormondom has had its share of "super women." With a tendency to make unrealistic demands upon themselves, many of these non-stop workers produce large families, participate in Church activities, and maintain high homemaking standards, in addition to meeting professional demands. Some admit that they often over-compensate to avoid failure because when they compromise their high standards in any area, they must cope with their feelings of guilt.

With sewing established as a cultural tradition for women since the days when Brigham Young confronted them with such questions as "How many sisters here are wearing clothes made by their own hands?," a Mormon woman lawyer today expresses regret that she cannot manage to take her children to Sunday School in home-sewn clothes. This would be an unlikely concern of women lawyers outside the kingdom. Reflecting another deep-seated tradition, a Latter-day Saint woman with work outside the home allowed that she is "cheating" if she hires household help. And Mormon women have always been uncomfortable with hiring baby-sitters as Elizabeth Cady Stanton observed in 1871:

That thoroughly democratic gathering in the Tabernacle impressed me more than any other Fourth of July celebration I ever attended. As most of the Mormon families keep no servants, mothers must take their children wherever they go—to churches, theatres, concerts, and military reviews—everywhere and anywhere. Hence the low, pensive wail of the individual baby, combining in large numbers, becomes a deep monotone, like the waves of the sea, a sort of violoncello accompaniment to all their holiday performances. It was rather trying to me at first to have my glowing periods punctuated with a rhythmic

95

wail from all sides of the hall; but as soon as I saw that it did not distract my hearers, I simply raised my voice, and, with a little added vehemence, fairly rivaled the babies.

Stanton wrote that she commented on this trial to one of the theatrical performers, who replied:

It is bad enough for you, but alas! imagine me in a tender death scene, when the most profound stillness is indispensable, having my last gasp, my farewell message to loved ones, accentuated with the joyful crowings or impatient complainings of fifty babies.[13]

Of course, Mormon women easily can develop the superwoman syndrome without an outside profession. With homemaking the Mormon specialty, it carries such high expectations that women caught up in the home-Church complex are hardly likely to become ladies of leisure. Husbands working as unpaid clergy for the Church still spend many hours away from home, leaving wives with a heavy load. As the real providers on the home front, the sisters consider it their duty to be perfect mothers and devoted helpmates, excellent cooks and gracious entertainers, fine seamstresses and immaculate housekeepers, as well as diligent Church workers. If ever it can be said that women are expected to be all things to all people, it can be said of the women of Mormondom.

In an interview with George W. Cornell, religious editor of the Associated Press, in 1974, former Relief

Society President Belle Spafford said that "Mormon women who are serving are not frustrated women wondering what to do to occupy themselves." Indeed, many Mormon women are frustrated women because they have too much to do. While some accept their duties more willingly than others, almost every woman I interviewed commented about the heavy demands of the culture. Only in the Mormon Church could women be suspicious of acquiring the priesthood because it would involve more work. As explained in Chapter 2, instead of yearning for it, they laughingly scream in protest, "Who would want it!" That actually is not the reason they don't pursue the priesthood, as we have seen. It is an "in-joke" shared by women of the culture that reveals their tension.

The demands made upon the Mormon homemaker are not always a subject of humor, however, and are often overwhelming. In their struggle to measure up to the high standards, many women in the culture experience considerable life-stress. Of those I have interviewed, several lament that domestic failures, especially those involving children's behavior, are accepted as personal failures, and while some look to the Church for understanding and support, others view their fellow church members as their harshest critics. In their race toward perfection the Mormons often measure themselves against each other, sometimes creating a competitive atmosphere within the Church.

Of course, competition is no stranger to success-oriented Americans, but the pressures of competing for religion-related success in Mormon group life are viewed by some as unusual enough to warrant psychiatrists for Mormons only. Success could not be guaranteed for such specialized professionals, however, because the belief in psychiatric counseling has not been popular among the disciplined, self-sufficient Mormons. "For one thing," one member explained, "people in the Church are reluctant to talk about their feelings honestly because there is an expectation about how they *should* feel."[14]

In an article printed in the *Journal of Operational Psychiatry* in 1977, Rodney W. Burgoyne, M.D., and Robert H. Burgoyne, M.D., psychiatrists with extensive experience among the Mormons, confirm the Saints' reluctance to seek psychiatric help.

...Mormon women are often in conflict and depressed. But in church teachings they are told they are happier and healthier than most other women and, if they are worthy, will be able to handle adversity because of their strength and God's help. To be overtly in emotional trouble, therefore, exceedingly undermines self-esteem. To seek psychiatric help is an admission of personal failure far beyond that of the non-religious person, and is usually done either secretly or with permission of some church authority with whom counseling has failed.[15]

In the article the Burgoynes also discuss the complexities of treating troubled Mormon women. They note that proper management of patient members of such cultures "demands cognizance of the magnitude of this institutionally produced stress"—an understanding of the *depth* of their tradition and commitment to the Church. The authors warn, however, that criticism of the patient's belief structure or suggestion that her anger or depression is a result of her attempt to live "impossible" church principles can be hazardous, because it could prevent the establishment of a trusting patient relationship. On the other hand, they note that a psychiatrist who seems overly sympathetic to the Church can prevent the patient from expressing her anger and can intensify her guilt.

In such a demanding culture, people sometimes find it difficult to recognize their weaknesses and admit their failures, but if the Latter-day Saint women do not readily accept weakness, many accept instead chronic headaches, problems with overweight, and a variety of psychosomatic illnesses. There is no decisive evidence to document their opinions, but several Utah physicians have suggested that such problems are expecially prevalent among Mormon women. Whether the alcoholism and high suicide rate among women in Utah or the serious problem with child abuse in the state can be related to pressures of Mormonism is not clear, but they are indicators that Zion has its share of problems.

Convinced they should "count their blessings" instead of complain, Mormons have learned to affect the conforming Church facade of "lollipops and rose gardens," as one woman phrased it. The ability to conceal problems while simultaneously presenting a public show of strength and cheerfulness is considered by many to be a highly admirable quality. But some critics of the Mormon culture view this practice among the Saints as widespread hypocrisy. However, if the women of the culture have been silenced or publicly intimidated by the Church or their priesthood-holding husbands, the sisters over the years readily have acknowledged their expertise in manipulative games. From confidences shared in diaries and letters of yesterday, and from exchanges among women of today, again with an element of humor, it is apparent that Mormon women have learned their own effective methods of coping with their position of strength without power. One auxiliary leader is quoted as saying, "We think up the ideas and give them to the men, and then they present them back to us as their own ideas."[16]

The cultural tradition of the domineering Mormon woman using indirect methods to influence a "strong" husband to whom she is supposed to be submissive has been formalized in the book *Fascinating Womanhood* (1965) by Mormon woman Helen B. Andelin. In her book Andelin proposes a strategy that is a combination of "sauciness and steel velvet," and suggests playfully pouting or stomping the foot as effective means by which a woman can get her own way. The more sophisticated Mormon women no doubt would reject the Andelin techniques and instead would approach the problem with more subtlety.

There is no question that the Mormon sisters frequently gain the upper hand with their matriarchal underground operations, particularly in the domestic domain, but their surface image, nevertheless, involves some denial of feelings, an acceptance of what is to be, and a "stiff upper lip." Perhaps this characteristic of the sisterhood provides a clue to the remaining mystery of how Mormon women living in polygamy not only tolerated but cheerfully endorsed the system that oppressed many of them. Much of the courage and strength that Mormonism has cultivated in its women have been channeled into endurance.

With American society wallowing in self-indulgence, certainly a measure of endurance and self-sacrifice deserves some respect, and if Mormon women are better equipped than others with that capacity, it is much to their credit. However, the extent to which a woman feels duty-bound to endure difficult situations at the expense of personal fulfillment has been a very interesting question connected with the feminist movement. In advocating that women relinquish their roles as servants, feminism indeed has presented a counter influence and created a dilemma for church women whose very existence has been linked with service. But again, the philosophy

101

of feminism is often distorted by its enemies and even by some of its friends. If a woman derives her greatest pleasure from serving others, and does so by her own choice, it would be entirely consistent with feminist philosophy. What is not consistent with feminist philosophy is for women to accept the male voice, including the church patriarchy, dictating what they should do.

Had it not been for the women's movement, the plight of the Latter-day Saint woman might not have emerged so rapidly as a shortcoming of the kingdom. As feminists of the nation began insisting that women be recognized as individuals and demanding opportunities to meet women's diversified needs, some Mormon women began taking note that "the messages from the Mormon hierarchy are the same for all women, not individualized," and complaining that "they conform to some very limited role notions."[17]

Of course, Mormon women have their free agency, they are told, but Mormon free agency is described by one woman as working like a father-child relationship. "The church fathers tell you what is right on an issue [its connection with morality is often remote], and then you know you can go ahead and do the wrong thing if you choose, but you will receive disapproval for your actions."[18]

By this method, conforming has become accepted as normal and "good" in the culture, and being different a flaw or weakness. While the Church takes pride in welcoming everyone to conform to its teachings, several women I have talked with point out that it is also quick to ostracize those who don't accept the offer. "If you don't want to lose credibility in the Church," explained one member, "you don't oppose the stand it takes."[19] Once discriminated against for its radical non-conforming ways, the Mormon Church, in demanding its own conformity, is accused now by critics within and without the organization of being highly discriminatory itself.

If women all conform to the restricted role of stabilizers of the kingdom, what is to become of the innovative spirit with which the Saints have been associated? Creativity is said to require individuality and even a measure of divergence, if you will. Given the strong Mormon work ethic, productivity is inevitable, but must all the creative energy in women be diverted into Church-sanctioned duties? This also is spoken of by Mormon women as a disconcerting problem. They fear that if the Relief Society dispenses enrichment from the central office in the form of packaged arts and crafts, Heloise household hints, and pre-interpreted literature, it will foster in its members a paint-by-number mentality. While Mormon women traditionally have been admired for their fine handicraft skills, many of the more discerning sisters recall the disturbing phenomenon of the 1960s when hundreds of Mormon coffee tables across the valley, prohibited from functioning as originally intended,* displayed Relief Society-inspired, home-crafted plastic grapes, the ultimate in kitsch by serious design standards.

In a university program featuring a discussion of western American literature, the question was posed to the mostly Mormon audience, "Instead of a native Utahan, why did it take an outsider, Edward Abbey, to capture the magnificence of the Utah landscape in the book *Desert Solitaire?"* Knowing laughter rippled through the audience when a voice responded, "Because we're too busy." Mormons are not certain that their God would approve of such unrestricted contemplation of the landscape, which borders on idleness.

It is not easy for a devout Mormon woman to turn the beauty of a summer day into painting or poetry when the peaches are ripe and ready to be canned. Utah certainly must be the canning capital of the world and the only place where canning fruit can be directly related to eternal salvation. There is no lack of talent among the women of the Mormon culture, but many potentially creative individuals settle for becoming mere dabblers, their talents compromised and energies diluted by going in too many directions at once. Many have noted the irony that Mormon society often hinders creativity while simultaneously

*Mormons prohibit the use of coffee, tea, alcohol, and tobacco.

claiming to nurture it. By its very design, the system intended to produce excellence seems destined to foster mediocrity.

In creating his hypothetical utopia in *Walden Two*, behaviorist B.F. Skinner presents a tension-producing mental exercise for some of his readers. The society he suggests is highly structured, but is an intelligently administered and fair society designed to meet basic human needs. Free to make some choices within the tight framework, the people are portrayed as both productive and happy. This Skinner-type utopia has appeal for many, but, of course, such a highly controlled society, even though its flaws are not apparent, seems too confining for those who place a high value on freedom. *Walden Two* makes such readers uncomfortable as they imagine themselves as participants in the society. They experience a strong desire to "pop out of their slots," the graphic description used by folklorist J. Barre Tolken to describe the non-conforming members of a culture. In the Mormon culture, as in *Walden Two* or any other well-ordered, conforming society, the majority are comfortably situated in their slots. But there are some unyielding members who keep popping out, and others, lacking momentum, who come crawling and sneaking out. An unknown number feel locked in and remain constantly squirming at the bottom of their slots, and because women's slots are smaller and more confining than men's slots, some of them are stuffed in so they can't move. Squashed under the pressure of oughts and shoulds, of obey and conform, they find themselves truly in a bind.

The gift of free agency has given the Mormons the freedom to be perfect, but not the freedom to be free. Because of their strong work ethic, the Mormons have not cultivated weak women who are pampered and placed on a pedestal. Instead they have produced a culture of strong women with no place to go.

She (woman) is defined and differentiated with reference to man and not he with reference to her; she is the incidental, the inessential as opposed to the essential. He is the Subject, he is the Absolute—she is the Other.

Simone de Beauvoir
The Second Sex

5

RELIEF SOCIETY: SISTERHOOD OF THE BROTHERHOOD

If history ultimately gives a fair and honest account of the roles women have played in its making, certainly the sisters of the Mormon Relief Society will stand out as remarkable contributors to the settling of the American West. The history of the organization itself, however, reflects a complex mix of female strength and resourcefulness with female submissiveness in a male authoritarian culture, which has given rise to much speculation about which stereotype most appropriately suits its members.

From the beginning, the priesthood leaders of the Church have established the general policies and goals for the women's Relief Society, although the women through the years have been given freedom, in varying degrees, to initiate and execute programs for achieving the male-defined goals. Patterned after the Church in its governmental structure, the women's auxiliary has leadership on the ward, stake, and general levels, with male authorities serving as their advisors on every level. This Mormon organization provides an extraordinary communication system: messages from the top authorities can be disseminated to the membership through this leadership network at a rapid rate and the women of the Relief Society can be easily mobilized to serve the needs of the kingdom.

It is unusual for women's organizations, including church auxiliaries, to have their officers selected by men, which is the case in the Mormon Church. The press reported that there were "sighs of surprise and disappointment" at the 1974 Church conference when President Spencer Kimball "released" the revered Belle Spafford as Relief Society president, an office she had held for thirty years, and named a new president, but few who were present would have questioned his right to do so. It was also the prerogative of the male President to appoint the two new counselors and the thirty-six-member general Relief Society board, just as it is the regular responsibility of ward bishops to select the Relief Society leaders on the local ward level. Although this practice is generally accepted today, the selection of Relief Society leaders was not designated as a function of the priesthood in the beginning, nor has it ever been specifically *revealed* as such.

Joseph Smith himself organized the first Mormon "Female Relief Society" in Nauvoo, Illinois, in 1842, just twelve years after the Church was founded. Defining its purpose at the first meeting, Joseph told the women he had in mind that

... the Society of the sisters might provoke the Brethren to good works in looking to the wants of the poor, searching after objects of charity and in administering to their wants; to assist by correcting morals and strengthening the virtues of the community, and save the Elders the trouble of rebuking, that they may give their time to other duties.[1]

At that meeting Joseph proposed that the *women elect* a president, and that *she* choose two counselors to assist in the duties of her office. After reassuring the sisters that he would give instructions from time to time if they needed them, he left the group, and the eighteen original Relief Society members then elected their own officers, choosing Emma Smith, Joseph's wife, for president.

The Prophet was there to supervise the organization of the first Relief Society, but forming the women's group had not been his idea. One of the sisters, Sara M. Kimball, recorded the circumstances that led to its establishment. She wrote in her journal that she invited some of the sisters to her parlor to consult on the subject of forming the ladies' society. Upon deciding to organize, the women called upon Sister Eliza Snow to write a constitution and by-laws that would be submitted to Joseph Smith prior to their first meeting. Eliza obligingly carried out the request, but when she presented the constitution and by-laws she had written to the Prophet, he said to her, "They are the best I have ever seen, but this is not what you want." He explained:

Tell the sisters their offering is accepted of the Lord and He has something better for them than a written constitution. Invite them all to meet with me and a few of the Brethren in the Masonic Hall over my store next Thursday afternoon, and I will organize the sisters under the Priesthood after a pattern of the Priesthood.[2]

When the women assembled, Joseph, along with two of the brethren, seated himself on a platform before the group and made the following pronouncement:

... Let this presidency serve as a constitution, all their decisions be considered law and acted upon as such.[3]

If that statement was ambiguous about which presidency he meant, the source of governing policy was defined clearly when Smith appeared at a subsequent meeting on April 28, 1842. At that time he advised the sisters:

You will receive instructions through the order of the Priesthood, which God has established through the medium of those appointed to lead, guide, and direct the affairs of the Church.[4]

After settling the matter of Relief Society leadership, Joseph elaborated on the duties of the organization. Perhaps the meeting followed one of his many rumored domestic squabbles with Emma because his counsel to the sisters was the following:

Let this society teach the women how to behave toward their husbands, to treat them with mildness and affection. When a man is borne down with trouble, when he is perplexed with care and difficulty, if he can meet a smile instead of an argument or murmur, it will calm down his soul and soothe his feelings.[5]

The day the Mormon women accepted Joseph Smith's principle of government, they relinquished the power over their own organization to the male priesthood holders of the Church. Of course, few women in 1842 would have been concerned about power in the Church, and in fact, for women to have been organized under the priesthood and directed by it was considered a privilege then, as it is today, by the majority of the sisters. Many of them have expressed gratitude for the guidance of the male authorities through the years, often repeating a statement Joseph Smith made to the original Relief Society group. "This Church," he said, "never was perfectly organized until the women were thus organized."[6] This has been interpreted consistently by Latter-day Saints as the way in which Mormon women were "elevated to their rightful place." Compared to the relatively inactive role of women in most religions of the nineteenth century, the organization of women's activities under the auspices of the Church was thought to be progressive for the times.

The Nauvoo Relief Society, which laid the groundwork for the existing organization, was terminated after the murder of the Prophet in 1844. After the disrupted Mormon colony migrated to Utah and settled new communities, local women's groups were formed, but it was not until 1867 that the Relief Society was resumed under Church leadership. Its reorganization then was instigated by Brigham Young, who, in proceeding with the awesome task of building a successful kingdom, foresaw a variety of reasons for such an organization to exist.

With the approaching completion of the transcontinental railroad in the late 1860s, the comfortable Mormon isolation was ending and the economic well-being of the community was threatened. The railroad had been introducing "outsiders" to the kingdom, among whom were merchants who promoted the latest American fashions. As Mormon women became tempted by what Brigham called "needless and fashionable imports," he envisioned that the diminishing of capital funds for such indulgences would have an adverse effect upon the local economy.

Brigham Young's discourses at that time on the subjects of women's extravagance, fashions of the times, and the arts of domestic economy indicate the extent of his concern with this problem—concern that ultimately led to his direction of women's activities altogether. In one such discourse, he admonished:

... our daughters are following vain and foolish fashions of the world. I want you to set your own fashions. Let your apparel be neat and comely, and the workmanship of your own hands. Wear the good cloth manufactured in our own mills and cease to build up the merchant who sends your money out of the Territory for fine clothes made in the East. Make your garments plain, just to clear the ground in length, without ruffles or panniers or other foolish and useless trimmings and styles.[7]

Always eager to lend his support to the teachings of Brother Brigham, counselor Heber C. Kimball sternly reprimanded the guilty sisters:

Where did you get your bonnets? Were they made here? No, they were made in the States. They came by succouring those poor curses who would send us all to destruction, by nourishing these Gentile merchants here. The best of them would sell this whole people for ten dollars, and permit my life and Brigham's life to be taken in a minute.[8]

Assuming the mantle of universal knowledge, Brigham gave endless instructions to women about activities that would keep the kingdom functioning smoothly at that time of economic stress. He advised them on efficient methods for keeping house, cooking meals, baking bread, and tending cows and pigs. There were suggestions from the prophet on the training of young girls to be good wives as well as on the washing and dressing of children.

Girls, learn to comb your hair in the morning. Wash your face nice and clean, and your neck; put on your dress comely, and make it look neat and nice. I do not mean protruding out behind like a two-bushel basket. When you come down the stairs, look as if you were wide awake, and not as if your eyes needed a dash of water to wash them clear and clean.[9]

President Young obviously recognized that the formal organization of women for channeling their economic and social activities into useful group enterprises would be beneficial to the kingdom. In 1865, when he was launching his campaign for the exclusive use of homemade products with local materials, the prophet made the suggestion that there be an "organization of sisters against purchasing goods at the store." He asked, "How many ladies present have made the ribbons they wear? The time is at

114

hand when you must make them or do without them." He told them he loved to see the human form adorned, but if they were organized into groups they could

... manufacture from straw, grass, or any other fitting material that grows in these valleys, bonnets and hats, and cease to sell the barley, the oats, the wheat, etc. to buy imported ones, or when the wheat, oats, and barley are all sold to get your husbands to run into debt, for that which you can as well make yourselves.[10]

According to their leader's suggestion, many of the sisters began to organize "female home manufacturing societies," but these societies did not become general and unified until direct counsel was given at the Latter-day Saints general conference in the Salt Lake Tabernacle in 1867. There, Brigham, in his official capacity as Prophet, said:

If the ladies would get up societies by which they could promote home labor of their sex, they would do what was well pleasing in the sight of heaven.[11]

Shortly thereafter, Brigham Young appointed his wife, Eliza R. Snow, to supervise the establishment of the "Female Relief Society" in every Mormon settlement, and he notified the bishops to organize branches in every ward. Eliza drew from her experience as secretary of the original Nauvoo Relief Society in carrying out her assignment, and within a

115

year, Relief Societies had been organized throughout the kingdom.

There was no mention of the women electing their own officers then, however, nor was that possibility considered when the central organization of the Relief Society was established in 1880. At that time Eliza Snow, who had led the organization for thirteen years, was simply sustained as president and two counselors and a staff of advisors were appointed by President John Taylor, who by then had succeeded Brigham Young. And since then it apparently has been assumed by Mormons that the women leaders should be appointed by male authorities. It is interesting, however, that in 1880, Eliza Snow had the authority to nominate Louise B. Felt for Primary* president and Elmira G. Taylor to head the newly formed Young Ladies' Mutual Improvement Association, positions which, since then, also have been appointed by male authorities.

While the original Relief Society purpose of charity again was emphasized by Brigham Young, his more important and clearly defined motive for the reactivation of the women's group was to mobilize women into useful economic programs for the Church. He made it known that he wanted them "to enlarge their sphere of usefulness for the benefit of society." In an article entitled "Economic Role of

*Primary is the Mormon organization for children.

Mormon Women," Latter-day Saint historian Leonard Arrington outlined five major tasks that were assigned to and carried out by the Relief Society in the late nineteenth century and contributed significantly to the Mormon economy. Each of the programs given to the women as a mission was designed to assist the kingdom by diminishing consumption and increasing production. In all cases the projects were conceived by the male church authorities who also gave direction to the women for their execution. At this point in their history, however, in responding to the interesting opportunities thus offered them, Mormon women demonstrated the strength and ingenuity that women can contribute to such endeavors. This we shall see as we briefly examine these productive episodes in the lives of the early Relief Society women.

With women's extravagance as his chief concern, Brigham called for a specific movement of "Retrenchment" as the Relief Society's first assignment. In preparing the sisters for this new commitment, he scolded them in the manner of the authoritarian father with little children:

I am weary of the manner in which our women seek to outdo each other in all the foolish fashions of the world. For instance, if a sister invites her friends to visit her, she must have quite as many dishes as her neighbor spread on a former occasion, and indeed she must have one or two more in order to show how much superior her table is to her neighbors'.[12]

He told the women that their silly rivalry also produced a habit of extravagance in food that had put fathers and husbands in debt. "The poor," he said, "groan under the burden of trying to ape the customs of those who have more means."

When he spoke of contemporary fashions, Brother Brigham not only advised against them, but he ridiculed them in such a way that it was surprising indeed that even a few women in the Mormon community continued appearing in such fashions. The popular "Grecian bend" style, according to his description, gave women humps on their backs that "make it so you can't tell a lady from a camel." He told the ladies they could do as they pleased about this fashion, but he warned them that if it were adopted, "I'm afraid our children will be born with humps."[13] He complained that the mutton-leg style took seven yards for sleeves and three for the dress, and pointed out that long trains, besides wasting cloth, would drag up dirt and raise a dust. He continued his mockery:

If I were a lady I would not have eighteen or twenty yards to drag behind me so that if I had to turn around I would have to pick up my dress and throw it after me, or just as a cow does when he kicks over the milk pail, throws out one foot to kick the dress out of the way. That is not becoming, beautiful, or convenient. You would think there was a six-horse team traveling there with a dozen dogs under the wagon.[14]

Assuring the sisters that this was not modesty, gen-

118

tility, or good taste, Brigham said such behavior didn't belong to a lady, but to an "ignorant, extravagant, or vain-minded person who knows not true principle."

The President decided that his own family should set an example and lead out in retrenchment. He gathered them together and proceeded in his own style of democracy.

We are about to organize a Retrenchment Association, which I want you all to join, and I want you to vote to retrench in your dress, in your tables, in your speech, wherein you have been guilty of silly, extravagant speech and light-mindedness of thought.[15]

Accordingly, the Young family members voted to support retrenchment and "it was settled that night that Spartan plainness of dress was to be one of the distinguishing marks of the new movement."

Again, Eliza Snow was appointed to organize a program and carry the plan to the Relief Societies throughout the Territory, and the Saints responded favorably. Soon, throughout Zion, there were retrenchment associations for young ladies as well as retrenchment departments of the Relief Society for the older women. Having made their formal commitment, these groups resourcefully managed to keep the lid on extravagant spending until after the economic crisis that had threatened the kingdom subsided. Strict retrenchment was abandoned in 1877, but the organization for young women remained as the Young Ladies' Mutual Improvement Association, adopting general self-improvement as its purpose.

Concurrent with retrenchment, the second assignment given to the newly-formed Relief Societies called for the operation of cooperative general stores. The two-fold purpose behind these Church-operated stores was to provide a market for Mormon products and to use the profits for local investments. The Mormon sisters were counseled to set up retail outlets for their own handwork, to patronize them exclusively, and even to buy stock in them. Thus, beginning in 1869, cooperative stores began springing up throughout Utah Territory, many of which were set up and were completely managed by Relief Society members. Dressmaking departments were featured in some stores while others specialized in millinery, and most served as centers of exchange for locally manufactured products.

The most successful of the cooperative stores was the "Women's Cooperative Mercantile and Manufacturing Institution," which opened in 1876 near South Temple and Main Street in Salt Lake City, now the location of Z.C.M.I.,* one of America's oldest department stores. In requesting the establishment of this store, Brigham Young sent a letter to the Relief Societies in the Salt Lake area which suggested, "If you cannot be satisfied with the selection of sisters from among yourselves to take charge, we will render you

*Z.C.M.I. stands for Zion's Cooperative Mercantile Institution.

120

assistance by furnishing a competent man for the transaction of the financial matters of this establishment."[16] But the women from the area managed ably without the help of a male. They sold their homemade products there on commission, including staple dry goods, ladies' furnishings and ornamentation, knit underwear, and children's wear. Stores modeled after this fine business enterprise were set up in several cities in Utah Territory, all of which were operating at the turn of the century, and the church officials were reported to have been pleased indeed at the way these establishments had contributed to the economy by "keeping the money in the Territory."

With the retrenchment and cooperative merchandising missions well underway, the Latter-day Saint leadership then began promoting additional projects for the Relief Society under the general category of "home industry." Through the *Woman's Exponent* the word went out to the sisters of their new assignment from the prophet Brigham:

Every branch of the Relief Society is called upon to lay hold of this subject of home industry with a will, and to take active part in the great work of bringing about the perfect organization of a self-sustaining people.[17]

A large variety of industries was suggested, but the notion of women being "self-sustaining with respect to clothing" again was emphasized as being of prime importance. Thus, the women and girls continued to

121

be directed toward clothing-related endeavors especially. Wool and cotton by that time were being manufactured in Utah, and women who could outfit themselves and their families from head to toe from their own labors using Zion's own materials were the most valued sisters of the kingdom. Some of the sisters still had a taste for finery, however, and Brigham determined that if women were going to insist upon wearing silk, it would be necessary for them to produce it themselves rather than importing it.

Actually, Church leaders had been attracted to the silk industry since 1865, but it was not until 1875, after the woman's home industry movement had been launched, that they placed official responsibility for its development upon the Relief Society. Sister Zina D.H. Young was given the mission of establishing the silk industry by her husband Brigham Young, which turned out to be somewhat unfortunate. It was with considerable difficulty in "overcoming her great repugnance to silk worms"[18] that Sister Young succeeded in fulfilling her assignment. Nevertheless, through her efforts and courage, a "Deseret Silk Association" was formed by Relief Society leaders for the purpose of purchasing cocoons, distributing eggs, and giving instructions for raising worms and reeling silk. And within a year after the new Relief Society project began, Utah Territory was literally crawling with silk worms, with the sisters solemnly resolving to delay satisfying their need for fine clothes until their own Zion-made silk was available.

With the land abundantly covered with mulberry leaves, furnishing shade and food for an estimated five million silk worms, a formal resolution was offered by Brigham Young and was unanimously approved in the April 1877 general conference of the Saints "that all Relief Societies throughout the Church take a mission to raise silk and do all in their power to clothe their families." Four months after the official adoption of the plan, death claimed the Prophet Brigham, but his counsel to raise silk had been accepted by the Relief Society as "a special revelation to the sisters." Therefore, the industry continued, and with missionary zeal the women planted ten thousand new mulberry trees, conducted classes and lecture tours, and imported special machinery for their work. Leonard Arrington has noted that Susanna Cardon, a Relief Society stalwart from Logan, Utah, acquired such expertise as a "reeler" that she was "called on a mission" to teach the art throughout the Territory. Sister Cardon left a one-year-old baby along with six other children to provide instruction without pay for the Church. In turn, some of the women and children she taught were appointed as missionaries to pass the skill on to others.

The truth about the Utah silk industry is that it was not very profitable in the long run, and it never was very popular. In fact, the activity created havoc in many Mormon households as the worms began to occupy two or three rooms of the house. Diligent sisters requested several ounces of eggs, but from each ounce of eggs many large worms emerged. In some cases the entire family had to be activated to gather enough leaves to feed the voracious worms and to provide clean trays and controlled temperatures for them. To make matters worse, the worms gave out a most unpleasant odor.

In the article previously mentioned, Arrington included excerpts on the subject of sericulture from the minutes of the Relief Society of St. George, Utah, which suggested that even though the sisters were unfaltering in their devotion to their mission, the Saints had a certain amount of skepticism about the value of the project. In May 1878 it was recorded that a Sister Snow from that ward said she undertook the business not for what she could gain, but "because it was obeying the counsel of the authorities and was building up Zion." She noted that "they (the worms) were not all that much trouble, as they didn't need their food cooked." In May 1880 the minutes said Sister Eyring admitted that she did not think they would make a great deal of money out of the silkworms. "But still," she said, "if we learn to handle them and plant the mulberry we are making that much progress in the Kingdom and doing our duty. We will get our reward, whether we make much or little," she reasoned.

The disruptive influence of the worms was reflected in the remarks of Bishop David H. Cannon that were included in the minutes as interpreted by the secretary.

He felt interested in the business, but would not labor as he has seen the sisters do to take care of them (worms) and get nothing for it. He would feed them to the chickens. Does not like to see the sisters go out into the fields and around and carry bundles of mulberry boughs on their backs.

The minutes of 1880 also mentioned that "some brethren were complaining that the women were turning the parlors over to the worms" and that "the smell of worms drove them from the house to eat in the woodshed."[19]

In spite of the adversities, the Church authorities surged ahead to expand the silk industry, establishing the Utah Silk Association on a financial basis, selling stock and acquiring factories with expensive imported machinery. Even then the business did not flourish. Apparently the machines were inferior and there was insufficient skilled labor to prepare the silk for the loom. Many dedicated sisters continued to carry out the complete process individually with satisfying results, nevertheless, and some became genuinely enthusiastic about the work.

The failing industry experienced one last revival at the time Utah achieved statehood in 1895. The legislature then established the Utah Silk Commission, with Relief Society leaders as its officers, and appropriated funds for sericulture. One of the officers of that commission, Mrs. Margaret Caine, presented a talk about sericulture in Utah at the meeting of the International Council of Women in London in 1898. But because the industry never seemed to progress beyond the experimental stage, resulting in the large-scale production of nothing but souvenir silk handkerchiefs, state aid was discontinued in 1905. The Commission and county associations were dissolved and the mulberry leaves and worms appropriately expired into oblivion.

Of historical significance, at least, was the presentation to Mrs. Rutherford B. Hayes of "an elegant white silk collarette" made of Utah silk by the Relief Society when she and President Hayes visited Salt Lake City in September 1880, and the presentation of a silk gown to suffrage leader Susan B. Anthony by Relief Society suffragists which she was reported to have worn when the Intermountain Woman's Suffrage Convention was held in Salt Lake City in 1895. Of the economic contribution to the community, Arrington noted that involvement in the industry "did much to dampen female demands for costly imported clothing." To that extent it might be concluded that the silk project was of value to the kingdom.

Perhaps this example of the Relief Societies' dutifully undertaking the care and feeding of worms epitomizes the extent to which the Mormon sisters have followed the guidance of the authorities of the Church. Even after it was apparent that the project was unproductive, the diligence of the "good" sisters in pursuing their ill-fated mission gained the praise and respect of the Church. Undoubtedly, there were a few non-conforming women who exercised intelligent and independent judgment against devoting their time to the odiferous little creatures from the beginning, but, in the Mormon community, such women probably would have been suspected of misusing their free agency and thus placing their eternal salvation in jeopardy.

A fourth and more successful collective endeavor of the Relief Society was grain-saving for the community. Latter-day Saints always had been counseled to be prepared for food shortages. Between the years 1847 and 1867, they had good cause for such considerations. But in later years, when the threat of starvation had subsided because of the coming of the railroad, the membership ceased to take the savings plan seriously enough to suit the church authorities. Despite warnings of famine, Brigham Young could not convince the men of the kingdom that they should refrain from selling all extra grain for cash. Therefore, the prophet decided to enlist the aid of the Relief Society for the task of grain-saving, this time calling Sister Emmeline B. Wells, editor of the *Woman's Exponent*, to lead the way. Brigham sent for Emmeline to come to his office after the Church Conference of October 1876. He explained to her that he had called upon the brethren to lay up grain against a day of want, but they wouldn't follow his advice.

Thus, he told Emmeline, "I want to give you a mission, and it is to save grain." He continued:

The brethren tell me that the sisters want them to sell the grain to buy bonnets and other finery. I want the sisters to save grain. I want you to begin by writing the strongest editorial that you can possibly write on the subject.[20]

If the sisters had been responsible for the problem, the sisters had the ability to solve it as well. As directed, Emmeline quickly published her strong editorial, organized a purchasing committee, and activated the Relief Societies into a most vigorous "Save the Grain" campaign. With proceeds from the sale of handmade items, benefit performances, and a variety of money-making schemes they devised, the women were able to purchase wheat, and they acquired more wheat by gleaning the "wasted harvest," that which remained on the ground after the brethren had harvested. In locating storage for their wheat, some groups managed to employ husbands and bishops to erect granaries, and within a year the Relief Society had accumulated 10,465 bushels of wheat and 7,358 pounds of flour and the resources to continue expanding the program.

So successful was the Relief Society wheat program that it continued well into the twentieth century. Besides supplying a comfortable food surplus, the wheat was lent for seed to farmers who were in economic difficulty, and when a severe drought hit southern Utah from 1898 to 1901, the Relief Society wheat proved helpful indeed. A carload of flour from the Mormon kingdom went to help the victims of the San Francisco earthquake and fire of 1906, and Mormon flour assisted those affected by the 1907 famine in China. Through the church leadership the Relief Society sold 200,000 bushels of grain at $1.20 per bushel to the United States Government in 1918 for aiding European allies during World War I, and the accumulated interest from investing that money in a trust fund provided the Relief Society with a sizable budget for their health and welfare projects.

The women were justifiably proud of their grain-saving project and, on several occasions, demonstrated, in fact, that they had become quite possessive of their grain. It seems that some of the bishops felt that their priesthood authority should entitle them to make the ultimate decisions regarding the distribution of the Relief Society wheat. However, Arrington acknowledged that, in one of the few recorded actions of resistance to the priesthood in their history, the Mormon women asserted their independence and verbally objected to the bishops usurping this power. The first presidency of the Church supported the women, and in 1883 the authorities informed the bishops that they were not to take possession of and disburse the Relief Society grain. The matter came up again ten years later, and again the top leadership notified the bishops that "they must not interfere with the Relief Society about the storing up the wheat." The question remains, would any action have been taken by the women had the first presidency's decision been on the side of the bishops? Would they have continued their mission?

The final significant assignment carried out by the Relief Society sisters in the formative years of the kingdom was in the field of health care. The emphasis by the church leadership was toward teaching women to be responsible for their own maternity and other health needs by training midwives and maintaining a hospital. This effort resulted in

...the most remarkable flowering of medicine among women during the second quarter century of the Mormon settlement of Utah, and the large territory about it, that ever existed in any one region on the face of the earth. . . . no concentration of women in medicine ever occurred proportionately to equal the number of women doctors among the pioneers of Utah.[21]

Again it was Brigham Young who steered women in this direction, not necessarily to provide them with an opportunity for a prestigious profession, but with his deep distrust of outside doctors, to keep medical care within the Mormon society. And, as he also pointed out, "this program would be liberating men for the more important work of building the kingdom." As the Mormon midwives who had trained in the East before they migrated to Utah grew older, it became apparent to Brigham that younger women must be trained to replace them. Therefore, he devised a plan which was presented in the *Woman's Exponent* in 1873. He asked

. . . that three women from each ward in Salt Lake City be chosen to form a class for studying physiology and obstetrics. Also that one woman from each settlement be sent to the city to study the same branches, and the Bishops see that such women be supported.[22]

For many years Brigham Young and the Mormons had not fully recognized the medical profession and preferred faith healing instead, but the Saints finally conceded that medical education was respectable and acknowledged their need for trained physicians. Thus, the Prophet called women with special qualifications and aptitude to go East to study medicine. Although he did not receive the enthusiastic response he had hoped for, a handful of women responded to his call. A few, such as Dr. Ellis Shipp, have been singled out for comment in a previous chapter, but there were other Mormon women medical students whose stories were equally impressive. Romania B. Pratt, for instance, left a nursing child and four other children to accept a mission to go to Philadelphia Women's Medical College, with the agreement that after her return to Utah in 1877 she would teach the art of midwifery and help to establish a hospital in Utah Territory.

Under the direction of the church presidency, the Mormon sisters' Deseret Hospital became a reality in

1882. Starting with twelve beds and reaching a total of fifty, the hospital was purchased by Relief Society fund-raising projects, donations, and Church appropriations. With their own Dr. Ellen B. Ferguson serving as resident physician and surgeon and the managing board composed of Relief Society officers, Deseret Hospital functioned primarily as a maternity home, emergency hospital, and women's medical training center.

In 1894, after thirteen years of admitting an average of one hundred patients a year, the hospital closed its doors because of the kingdom's financial instability at that time. However, it was there, in 1887, that the first official Utah nursing school was organized and the place where the one-year practical nursing program was devised that is still used today in many cities throughout the country. For many years after their hospital closed the Relief Society continued its nursing school operation and remained active generally in the health care of the Mormon community.

The above accounts describe only the five most important economic contributions of the Latter-day Saints Relief Society of the nineteenth century, but in addition to these major undertakings numerous smaller tasks were relegated to the sisters as well. They regularly relieved men of lighter jobs such as typesetting, operating the telegraph, and the running of creameries and cheese plants. They also found time to publish their newspaper, *Woman's Exponent,* and to attend to their charitable affairs. And the majority of these women were dedicated mothers who were raising larger than average-sized families at that time.

Mormon women of the nineteenth century left behind them a record of activities and economic contributions to their community which is very likely unexcelled in American history. Certainly, their extraordinary achievements are manifestations of women's potential in every aspect of life. But at the same time—and herein lies the paradox—the circumstances under which they achieved demonstrate the most extreme example of female submission to and acceptance of male authority. Regardless of their impressive range of activities, the position of Mormon women in their community in no way could be construed as one of equality.

Remarks such as the following indicate that the Mormon leadership actually did not regard women with the esteem for which many modern-day Saints proudly credit them. In expressing his own attitude as well as that of the prophet, Brigham's counselor Heber C. Kimball was condescending, to say the least:

I heard my leader (Brigham Young) say, the other day, that he can manage the affairs of this people and of the United States and all of Europe with more ease to his mind than he can listen to the little trifling complaints that women bring to him. A good deal of it is little peevishness. . . . You should be home gleaning wheat or

133

knitting when you are gadding about from one place to another.[23]

Even though Brigham Young convinced women they were capable of broadening their sphere, he made statements such as the following that betray his liberal image:

I do not believe in making my authority as a husband known by brute force but by superior intelligence—by showing them that I am capable of teaching them.[24]

And teach them he did—by offering a steady flow of dictatorial messages such as:

My young sisters, instead of sitting continually at the piano and getting the consumption, take hold and build up Zion. Learn to labor.[25]

Brigham Young ordered, reprimanded, and manipulated women into productivity for the good of the kingdom, and sanctioned any activity that contributed to his Mormon empire, regardless of the time required out of the home. Prospects of the previously discussed rewards and punishments in eternal life, of which they were constantly made aware, kept women willingly committed to the obedience principle. Still, obedience to the counsel of the Prophet Brigham led many women into productive and self-fulfilling activities.

The sense of identity and positive reinforcement

134

from Mormon group life, in this case from their women's organization, no doubt accounts in great measure for the unusual success of pioneer Mormon women. An interesting comparison can be made between the closely-knit sisterhood in Utah Territory and the many no less courageous women who were living more isolated lives on the plains of the Midwest at that time. As portrayed in the works of Willa Cather and other authors, the pioneer women of the American plains often experienced despair and emotional difficulties as a result of the extreme loneliness they suffered.

That the Latter-day Saints' Relief Society has operated effectively under the priesthood from the beginning must be recognized. Taking into account its 1842 beginning in Nauvoo, the Mormon group claims to be the oldest as well as the largest active women's organization in America. It has maintained membership in the International Council of Women since 1888, when, under direction of Church President Wilford Woodruff, Emily S. Richards became the first delegate and later a member of that group's general board. The Mormon sisters' active participation in the National Council of Women has continued also since the Relief Society became a charter member in 1891.

Expressing their "humiliation at not having a building of our own," the membership voted to acquire a Relief Society house in 1909. At that time President Lorenzo Snow told them the brethren did not want the sisters to buy land, but "they would give them a piece on which to build."[26] Upon receiving the land, the Relief Society acquired its first building. However, buildings for the sisters have become a thing of the past. The Relief Societies today are neither allowed to buy land nor given land on which to build. Instead, they are permitted the use of a room in the local ward house, and because they recently have been denied exclusive use of that room, some of the sisters today are expressing "humiliation at not having a room of their own."

The uniform course of study for the Relief Society was conceived in 1914 and has continued to provide direction for Mormon sisters throughout the world since that time. The course included theology, literature, and social science then, and many felt that the Relief Society provided a fine opportunity for women to learn and develop. As we have noted, however, the content of the lessons has undergone a change, becoming more limited in scope, and today some women object to the fact that they are supposed "to do what is spelled out in the manual." As the uniform lesson plans gradually become more uniform, some feel there is too little latitude for discussion and the exchange of ideas.

For many years those lessons were contained in the special *Relief Society Magazine* which replaced the *Woman's Exponent* as the sisters' mouthpiece in 1914. The magazine also included news, stories, craft ideas, and recipes, and in combination with the visiting teacher program which was initiated in 1916, helped keep the sisterhood working as a cohesive unit. Unfortunately for some, that cherished women's publication, with its circulation of nearly 500,000, was arbitrarily discontinued by Church authorities in 1969. An excerpt from one of the last issues of the doomed magazine expresses the women's obedient acceptance, if not enthusiasm, about the decision:

We realize, sisters, that the discontinuance of the magazine after fifty-six years, during which it has served the society well and been a source of inspiration, instruction, enlightenment and interchange of ideas, as well as providing an outlet for the creative writings of the women of the Church, brings feelings of sadness to our hearts. We must remember, however, that with the growth and expansion of the Church, changes must be anticipated, accepted, and adjustments to new ways and new programs made with willingness and faith in the inspiration that guides our leaders.[27]

Another declaration from the authorities came in the late 1960s, informing the Relief Society that the budget, which had been successfully operated by the women since the nineteenth century, was to be taken over by the general offices of the Church. In 1892 the Relief Society had been incorporated as a legal entity for a fifty-year period, which allowed the women to transact their own business, and since then they had functioned successfully with their annual dues and fund-raising projects. But now it was decided that the money raised by Relief Societies must be turned over to the bishops of the wards. If there was acceptance of that decision by some, there was also widespread complaining.

Regarding their recent loss of privileges, one member said, "The women were highly indignant." But she made the astute observation that "the sisters protested only among themselves, not to the proper authorities."[28] When I asked in my interviews why the women didn't make their antagonistic feelings on these matters known to the leadership, many expressed a sense of futility and their usual apprehensions about dissenting. They were primarily concerned with social ostracism, but they confirmed their realistic fear of excommunication for extreme dissent. "In a hierarchy, you do what you are told," one woman remarked with dismay.[29]

But of this rigidity and low tolerance for differing opinions within the women's auxiliary of the Church, one member had this to say:

If women were better at being honest with each other in Relief Society, some good things would happen. But everyone is so worried about offending someone else that you really don't share yourself.[30]

She explained that she had been taught that one of the purposes of the Society is to be a sisterhood, but "if a sisterhood only works for people on the same wave length, it fails."

Taking into consideration the Church power structure, a teacher in higher education said, in fact, that she did not see how it would be possible for Mormon women ever to make any changes or have any influence since "they robbed us of our magazine and we can't control our treasury." Speaking of that usurped treasury, some members I interviewed noted the long hours and great creativity that had been put in by the Relief Societies to earn their money. "It hit very hard with me," offered a discouraged participant, "when we were told we had to go to the bishopric for our funds."[31] Still another critic allowed that she could understand part of the reason why these changes were made, but complained, "They were not done with finesse. They were just put down as orders." To which she added, "I don't think you can keep that sort of thing going today."[32]

Such submissive reactions of the majority of Relief Society sisters to these cited examples of patriarchal authority would be questioned by many of today's women, but obedient behavior has always been in keeping with the philosophy of the Relief Society. In fact, in 1942, upon the occasion of its centennial, reflections and philosophical statements to that effect were clearly articulated in a booklet entitled *Centenary of the Relief Society, 1842–1942*. President Amy Brown Lyman, inadvertently expressing little confidence in the sisters to handle their own affairs, wrote:

Relief Society women share in the inspiration and blessings which came through the holy Priesthood. Today the Society, like all other organizations of the Church, whether composed of men or women, accepts and honors this authoritative supervision and guidance and thus is spared the misunderstanding and dissention which often occur in organizations which function without such directions.[33]

Mormon women are discouraged from patronizing organizations without the direction of the priesthood to which Sister Lyman referred. The centennial message they received from the Church leadership made that clear:

Members should permit no other affiliations either to interrupt or interfere with the work of the Society. They should give Relief Society service precedence over all social and other clubs and societies of similar kind. . . . Relief Society is sufficient for all general needs of its members. It is the greatest, most efficient women's organization in the world.[34]

In continuing to foster this type of exclusiveness in its women, the Mormon Church possibly has done itself a great disservice. According to some of its own members, the Church has rendered the Relief Society vulnerable and deserving of the criticism most frequently leveled against it. Although the Society is based on the principle of service, the daily selfless service of the sisters is primarily directed inwardly for the benefit of their own people. Some of the women whom I interviewed are discouraged at the Relief Society's "appalling lack of awareness and concern for the world beyond and the problems of those who exist outside the Mormon faith." If for some Mormon women the idea of Christianity is to bake a cake for a sister when she is down, it is also to turn her back on the major social problems that plague the world.

There are Mormon women who have not overlooked these deficiencies within their auxiliary group nor have they overlooked the fact that in their own organization, as in many other aspects of their lives, the same authoritarian power that once directed them into diverse and productive activities is now used to restrict, confine, and subdue them. One woman has said of this plight that "given some different direction," the members who object to the current policies "would come out of the woodwork."[35]

Nevertheless, a spokesperson of the Relief Society General Board said in my interview with her in 1975 that it has been her observation that "the majority of the Relief Society women are quite happy,"[36] and former president Belle Spafford assured the Associated Press in 1974 that "the very position of the Church in regard to women helps to build their feminine self-esteem, if they are living their religion." In fact, both Sister Spafford and her successor Barbara Smith boast that "Mormon women do not need the 'Women's Liberation Movement' because they have

141

always been liberated," and they insist that "Mormon women have always been equal to men," proudly citing the achievements of the nineteenth-century Relief Society as well as early suffrage in Utah as examples. Because early women's suffrage is so frequently cited as a manifestation of Mormonism's progressive policies toward women, in the next chapter we will examine the coming of the vote to the women of the Latter-day Saint Church.

The first step in the elevation of women under all systems of religion is to convince them that the great Spirit of the Universe is in no way responsible for any of these absurdities.

Elizabeth Cady Stanton

6

POLYGAMOUS

SUFFRAGETTES

Utah is a land of marvels. She gives us first polygamy, which seems to be an outrage against "women's rights," and then offers the nation a female suffrage bill, at this time in full force within her own borders. Was there ever a greater anomaly known in the history of society?[1]

Responding to the bewildering behavior of the Mormons, such were the sentiments of the non-Mormon press in the year 1872.

The Mormon women of Utah Territory were, in

143

fact, the very first in modern America to exercise suffrage, although Wyoming Territory preceded Utah by several months in passing the first suffrage bill. Seraph Young, niece of Brigham Young, cast the first vote on February 14, 1870, in a Salt Lake City municipal election, and the women of Utah voted in the general election in September of that year. Utah Mormons have taken great pride over the years in claiming that important national distinction.

Yet there were curious circumstances surrounding that historical event that justified the confused reaction of the American public. If polygamy and women's suffrage seem unlikely partners, an unraveling of the tale reveals that suffrage came to Utah more because of polygamy than in spite of it. And also because of polygamy, Mormon women, who became some of the country's most active and enthusiastic suffragists, were prevented from receiving widespread recognition for their contributions on behalf of the suffrage movement in America. Regardless of their vigorous participation in that movement, the unusual story of Mormon suffragists remains an anomaly in the pages of feminist history.

Among the various Mormon peculiarities which provoked a negative response from American Gentiles in the nineteenth century, polygamy was the least tolerated. The American public was initially shocked and alienated upon learning of Mormon polygamy, and most never became accustomed to the idea. Outsiders associated the Mormon practice with

144

female abuse and degradation. The Republican Party platform of 1856 named polygamy and slavery "twin relics of barbarism" and pledged to abolish both. The anti-Mormon sentiment that was generated by America's hostile reaction to polygamy, which certainly must be viewed as stranger than polygamy itself, had an interesting effect upon Mormon women, and in fact, played a major role in shaping their lives at that time.

Joseph Smith's revelation concerning polygamy was first introduced and secretly recorded in 1843. Section 132 of the *Doctrine and Covenants* described the revelation as a patriarchal order of marriage modeled after ancient Hebrew customs. Plural marriages of Abraham, Isaac, David, Solomon, and Jacob were cited as Biblical examples for men to follow, and the women had such female models as Sarah, Ruth, and Rachel. For Mormons, who considered themselves chosen people representing the Israelites of the last days, there was some logic in restoring the ancient marriage customs of Israel. It should be understood, however, that originally Joseph Smith emphatically condemned plural marriage. In the *Book of Mormon* (Jacob 2:24) was written, "David and Solomon truly had many wives and concubines, which thing was abominable before me, saith the Lord."

Although the inspiration for polygamy originated in the Old Testament, its revival through Smith's modern-day revelation contained some strictly Mormon innovations. In the beginning, this complex

145

plural marriage plan was closely linked with the Mormon polytheistic doctrine, "As God was once, we are now, and as He is, we can become." As I observed in previous chapters, according to their eternal marriage law Latter-day Saint males can become God-like rulers over their families in the hereafter. When polygamy was incorporated as part of the eternal marriage law, Mormon men, with their multiple wives, could produce multitudes of their own offspring and create for themselves a splendid kingdom indeed. The emphasis was on procreation, because the Latter-day Saints intended to build a mighty nation on earth and in the eternal world. According to Dennis Michael Quinn's study entitled *The Mormon Hierarchy, 1832–1932: An American Elite*, "religion was the pretext, power was the motive."

Included in the plural marriage revelation was a message for women as to how they should respond to such a startling idea in nineteenth-century America. Section 132 of the *Doctrine and Covenants* explained that a woman was to be instructed in the new law by her husband; ". . . then she shall believe and administer unto him or she shall be destroyed." On the other hand, as we have seen, in return for her submissive cooperation in the marriage plan a woman was assured that she would share in the spiritual rewards of the Celestial Kingdom of Heaven. The arrangement was promoted as a partnership of sorts.

While the revelation offered great promise for the

146

hereafter, a certain amount of mystery and scandal surrounded the onset of polygamy in the earthly Mormon settlements, with motives of Church leaders suspected by the public of being of questionable moral integrity. As early as 1832, a decade before the revelation was recorded and while the Church was centered in Nauvoo, Illinois, Mormons were reported to have been experimenting with plural marriage. Tales of romantic escapades of Joseph Smith and other Church dignitaries who had taken a variety of wives, including wives of other men, are discussed in *No Man Knows My History* by Fawn Brodie and in *The Mormons* by Thomas O'Dea. The latter relates the story of one able Mormon convert and mayor of Nauvoo, John C. Bennett, who "delighted in the new doctrine, which seemed to suit him admirably, and seduced any number of women under its protection." It was not until he and Joseph Smith pursued the same young woman, Nancy Rigdon, that they became estranged, which resulted in Bennett's subsequent excommunication from the Church.[2]

If Gentiles were offended by Mormon polygamy, so were many within the Church itself at first, especially women. Upon being instructed in the revelation, Eliza R. Snow, who later wholeheartedly endorsed polygamy, recorded her initial response in her journal:

In Nauvoo, I first understood the practice of plurality was to be introduced within the Church. The subject was very

147

repugnant to my educated feelings—so directly was it in opposition to my educated feelings that it seemed as though all the prejudices of my ancestors for generations past congregated around me.[3]

But most of the sisters, while indignant and horrified in the beginning, realized that, however repugnant, Church doctrine revealed by the Prophet was truth and must be endured. Therefore, plural marriage was accepted—readily by some and reluctantly by others—but nonetheless accepted as religious principle, even though no more than 20 per cent of the Saints actually became involved in the practice at its height. Polygamy became especially prevalent among men who were rising in the Church hierarchy. The acquiring of plural wives became a measure of a male's devotion to religious principles and of his ability to provide, and thus became associated with social and religious status. It is significant, however, that a few prominent stalwarts of the Church totally rejected the idea, including Emma Smith, Joseph's first wife. Their resistance to polygamy along with their other grievances resulted in a break with the main Church. Remaining in Nauvoo, this dissident group formed the Reorganized Church of Latter-day Saints.

Polygamy was an open secret among the Mormons until they moved westward to Utah. Shortly thereafter, the institution of plural marriage became stabilized and their secret was publicly declared Church policy at the Latter-day Saints conference of 1852. Of

148

course, from the beginning their secret had been discovered by fellow Americans, who assumed all along
that their behavior was immoral. But essentially
what existed in Utah by the time plural marriage was
made official was a group of people simply living according to their religious principles, and in their
piousness and temperance, they were generally models of Puritanism.

Their households and habits closely resembled
those of early New England, the area from which
many Mormons descended, and their attitudes
regarding the patriarchal family order, with the exception of plurality, were not unusual. Church leaders frequently made such traditional pronouncements as "Women are made to be led, counseled, and
directed," and it was accepted generally that plural
wives would adopt the female role of subordination
and obedience which was to be complemented by the
wise, benevolent guidance and protection of the
male. Theoretically, all wives were to be treated with
equal consideration, although Mormon diaries tell
tales of many broken hearts as husbands turned their
attentions to their new favorites. Still, according to
the religion, there was no justification for rejected
feelings. Brigham Young gave the melancholy sisters
little sympathy.

You sisters may say that plural marriage is very hard for
you to bear. It is no such thing. A man or woman who
would not spend his or her life in building up the kingdom of God on earth. . . is not worthy of God or his king-

149

dom, and they never will be crowned, they cannot be crowned; the sacrifice must be complete. If it is the duty of a husband to take a wife, take her. But it is not the privilege of a woman to dictate the husband, and tell who or how many he shall take, or what he shall do with them when he gets them, but it is the duty of the woman to submit cheerfully.[4]

The Saints, who were deeply devoted to their faith, practiced polygamy then because it was religiously right. During the time they practiced it, however, they suffered serious problems with their image. Because the American public had been concentrating on the scandal of polygamy, assuming women were in servitude and bondage, they remained oblivious or largely ignored the way in which the Mormon "subservient wives" had been contributing to the kingdom in its effort to remain economically self-contained. As we have seen, this development, which occurred simultaneously with polygamy, was an equally unique and interesting feature of the early Mormon society that had a profound effect upon the lives of Mormon women.

As a result of the Saint's ambitious proselytizing policy which was discussed in an earlier chapter, the polygamous husbands were frequently called away on Church missions, leaving women alone, sometimes for years at a time. Thus, in addition to the Relief Society's economic contributions that have been outlined, the sisters were expected by Church leaders to undertake a complete assortment of men's jobs while they were gone. Upon seeing that some of the kingdom's counting house attendants were needed for church missions, for instance, Brigham Young could press the women into action by determining that "Women make just as good mathematicians and accountants as any man and could do the business of any counting house," and in like manner, he assured them they were ideally suited for innumerable tasks as the need arose.

If the Gentiles were correct in their assumption that pioneer Mormon women were not exactly "liberated," the nature of life on the Mormon frontier at least had the advantage of allowing diversity in their lives. And if the Mormon sisters were not pampered and elevated to the pedestal like the idealized ladies of the East, this had less to do with their bondage in polygamy than with their importance to the work force. With the power of Mormonism as a means to eternal exaltation, Mormon women entered into polygamy willingly, and for the survival of the Church, they became vital community participants. Thus, born of economic necessity, the strong Mormon woman was emerging as a reality in direct contrast to the poor image of her that was spreading throughout the country.

An interesting variety of curiously distorted images of the Utah women was circulated in America in the late nineteenth century which is discussed at length in Gail Farr Casterline's master's thesis en-

151

titled, *In the Toils or Onward for Zion: Images of the Mormon Woman: 1852-1890*. It has been concluded that the lives of polygamous Mormon women were extraordinary in many ways, but they were hardly the ways the Gentiles imagined. Portrayed by numerous authors as downtrodden victims of male oppression and exploitation, the Latter-day Saint sisters were featured in newspaper articles, magazines, and over fifty full-length novels between 1852 and 1890, almost none of which were sympathetic to the Mormon culture. Male and female licentiousness was said to have been rampant in Mormondom, and tales of cruel "sister wives" were cited along with sensational accounts of suicides, escapes, and torture chambers. The high-principled Mormon sisters sometimes were depicted by novelists as depraved harlots or slaves. It was during this period that the evolution of the domestic novel was taking place in America, and a popular theme was that of good wives with straying husbands. The Mormon situation seemed to fit conveniently into that format, with the first wife usually featured as the tragic heroine.

Of course, with the Utah Territory geographically remote, as Casterline points out, very few of the fictional or nonfictional accounts were based on first-hand experience. And the preconceived attitudes of those who did visit Utah brought forth a wide variety of often contradictory reports about the Mormon situation there. A visit in 1872 from Mark Twain, who apparently found Mormon women less than ravishing, elicited this often quoted facetiousness:

I was touched. My heart was wiser than my head. It warmed toward the poor ungainly and pathetic "homely" creatures, and as I turned to hide the generous moisture in my eyes, I said, "No, the man that marries one of them has done an act of Christian charity which entitles him to the kindly applause of mankind, not their harsh censure, and the man that marries sixty of them has done a deed of open-handed generosity so sublime that the nations should stand uncovered in his presence and worship in silence.[5]

Richard Burton, who traveled through Utah Territory in 1860, was cited by Casterline as one of the few visitors who took a deeply critical look at the Mormon culture. Burton noted in his *The City of the Saints* that "womanhood (in Utah) is not petted and spoiled as in the Eastern States." Burton clearly condemned the American practice of restricting women by "making Goddesses of them," and he wrote that women such as those in Utah "seem happier than when set upon an uncomfortable eminence." Burton couldn't help remarking, however, about the distinct economic advantage he saw in plural marriage. "Servants are rare and costly," he said. "It is cheaper and more comfortable to marry them."[6]

Another astute observer of the Mormon scene was a woman visitor who came to Utah in 1872, Elizabeth

Wood Kane. In her published journal *Twelve Mormon Homes*, she recorded a sensitivity to the emotional difficulties that polygamy imposed upon women. In spite of their observable hardships, Kane nevertheless described Morman women as good-natured, industrious, and charitable. That marital bliss was sometimes lacking in Zion was confirmed in the books of two disenchanted Mormon wives themselves. Fanny Stenhouse wrote an angry account of polygamous life entitled *Tell It All*, and Ann Eliza Young, a former plural wife of Brigham Young, published a book called *Wife #19: Life in Mormon Bondage*. Ann Eliza had deserted her husband and Mormonism entirely after being assigned to run a farm on the outskirts of Salt Lake City to provide food for "sister wives" with no support from Brigham, and her story so captured the hearts of the American public that it became a best-seller. Her story also served to reinforce some of the Mormon critics' worst suspicions.

With an insatiable appetite, the American public consumed the vast quantities of published literature about the polygamous Mormon Saints. As Casterline suggested, possibly in what became almost a bizarre national preoccupation with the "evils" of polygamy, some of the more conventional Americans were provided a focus for their own frustrations that were centered in the shortcomings of monogamous life. Perhaps, as frequently is the case when there is excessive criticism, those who took a moralistic stand felt some identification with the subject upon which they dwelled, in this case the oppression of women.

Whatever was involved, it is clear that the popular nineteenth-century American conceptions of womanhood and marriage were not broad enough to include Mormon polygamy. The variety of experimental lifestyles that followed in the second half of the twentieth century would have been far beyond the comprehension of the Victorians of the 1800s. Despite America's claim to a democratic philosophy, Mormon polygamy seemed altogether "un-American." Although freedom was endorsed in America, there was, after all, a limit to the amount of freedom that could be tolerated. So contrary was polygamy to the mainstream of American thought, in fact, that Utah Territory, eagerly seeking admittance to the Union, was repeatedly denied statehood by the Congress because of it and the possibility of polygamy being outlawed by the United States government became a serious threat. Thus, the increasing pressure brought to bear against the Mormon way of life made it imperative for the Saints to defend their position against the unsympathetic Gentiles once again.

Who could better defend the Mormon marriage system than the polygamous wives themselves? Encouraged by Church authorities to defend their religious principles publicly, the Mormon sisters proceeded to do just that. And if they had ever matched their stereotype of weak, ineffectual

155

women, their concerted efforts to counteract that negative image cultivated in them the opposite qualities. Beginning in approximately 1870, the sisters of the Mormon Relief Society, in an institutional political maneuver, became outspoken advocates of women's rights. First and foremost, they indignantly charged that no woman should be denied her basic right to freedom in regard to her own marriage style. And in further defending their marriage style, the Mormon women presented several interesting arguments on its behalf. Their arguments, in fact, became so convincing, at least to themselves, that in a mind-boggling reversal they began speaking of themselves as happy, independent, virtuous women and of their unfortunate sisters who were locked into the wicked monogamous situation as the unenlightened victims of male oppression. Here, in this uprising of Mormon women in defense of polygamy, is perhaps the ultimate example of how women have been coerced, in the name of God, to participate in their own oppression; and in this case there was the ironic twist of the argument being presented under the guise of women's rights.

While the "feminist" arguments of Mormon polygamous wives hardly qualified as legitimate feminism, the sisters did make at least one rather reasonable and valid point which should not be lightly dismissed. Polygamy, they argued, served to liberate a woman because it made fewer demands upon her. Because wives could share child care and household duties, they said they had more time to develop additional skills and talents. After all, where else were mothers of little children free to go away to medical school? Pursuing a profession was not prohibitive for women who could leave their children at home with a "sister wife." Modern-day feminists, in their struggle for equal rights and liberation, are fond of saying, "Every working woman needs a wife at home." Many of the nineteenth-century Mormon women did, in fact, have at least one wife at home.

Reflecting Victorian attitudes toward sexuality, these busy plural wives also reasoned in their defense of plural marriage that they were protected from their husbands' lustful demands, whereas women in monogamy were always subject to their husbands' sexual desires. Again, the sisters claimed this as an advantage because it gave them more time to themselves, and also because it allowed the "proper continence during gestation to make healthier babies," a popular medical notion at that time. On this subject, Sister Martha Hughes Cannon, physician and Utah state senator, is often quoted as having said, "If her husband had four wives, one wife had three weeks of freedom every month."[7]

Monogamists were self-righteously defending the moral integrity of the country in vigorously opposing Mormon polygamy. Yet, again ironically, Mormon women argued *for* polygamy on the same grounds. They proudly pointed out how the option of taking plural wives eliminated male infidelity, which was

157

so common in the monogamous system. They readily admitted that men are naturally polygamous, but hastened to emphasize, on the other hand, that the idea of *women* having more than one husband was a "scandalous perversion of the natural order." "A true woman," they said, "could never love more than one man at a time." Mormon spokeswoman Helen Mar Whitney explained in her book *Why We Practice Plural Marriage*, "The love for one man exhausts and absorbs woman's whole conjugal nature."[8] Thus as Casterline observes, the Mormon polygamists saw justification of their beliefs both in religious doctrine and human nature. It might be said that the Mormons simply "institutionalized the double standard."

The point that plural wives were offered both freedom and security along with an opportunity for self-development must be conceded. Indeed, many unfulfilled women directed their energies to self-development by default. But their professing to an all-encompassing emotional commitment to a man who was to be shared raises the obvious question of jealousy, also an undeniable aspect of human nature. Of that problem, the sisters admitted it was sometimes difficult, but they rationalized the situation by explaining that coping with such difficulties helped to build good character. They held that in learning to overcome jealousy they also learned to love their neighbors as themselves, which was a sign of true spiritual progress.

158

From personal diaries, not official Mormon historical accounts, we learn that the polygamous life that
Mormon women endorsed was much kinder to some
than others. Many women actually adapted nicely
and thrived in the system and had been sincere in
their praise, but others, alone and destitute, were
sustained only by their faith. They were true religious martyrs whose stories were more compelling
than much of the fiction that was circulated.

It is not my intention here to engage in psychohis-
tory, but I would like to suggest that the following
entry in the diary of Ellis R. Shipp, M.D., which was
made only three weeks before her unanticipated
decision to answer Brigham Young's call for women
to go East to medical school, provides some insight
into why she made that decision. Ellis was living
with three other wives under one roof, not in
complete harmony, when she wrote:

Once I was happy for I thought I was beloved—Yes, I
thought I knew I was—probably I was then—but Oh, it is
past. I feel my heart breaking and I sigh o'er what has
been, but now has ceased to be. Even in my happiest
moments the thought that he would ever change was ago-
nizing and I felt that the realization of such an event
would deprive me either of my life or reason. Heaven
grant the result may not be so dreadful.[9]

In a collection of letters between two Mormon
friends, written in 1856 and 1857, again some very
understandable human emotions were expressed.

159

Ellen Clawson in Utah wrote to Ellen Pratt McGary in San Bernardino, California:

Just ten days ago Hyrum brought home a new wife. My heart is rather heavy. I never thought I could care again. I think perhaps Margaret (second wife) feels worse than I do for she was the last, and I suppose thought he would never get another, same as I did. And "misery loves company," you know.[10]

Ellen McGary in turn confided to her friend Ellen Clawson, ". . . should I believe one quarter what I hear about the doings up there (Salt Lake City), I should never dare to come there in my life." Although she was safe in California where an anti-polygamy law had been recently passed, Ellen Clawson warned her friend nevertheless, "If your husband is a true Saint, I might *possibly* be obliged to send the comforting words, 'grin and bear it' to you."[11]

No matter the hardships that were encountered, complaining certainly was not looked upon with favor by Church leaders. Indeed, the sisters were expected to "grin and bear it." At one point, Brigham Young said in despair, ". . . there is no cessation to the everlasting whining of many of the women in this Territory." Stories of "women being tied down, abused, and misused" were heard so frequently around the kingdom and, according to Brigham, so many women were "wading through a perfect flood of tears because of some men, together with their own folly," that he could tolerate it no longer. Thus, the Prophet called the membership together and, explaining that he "had to do something to get rid of the whiners," offered all the women of Mormondom their liberty. Beginning with his own collection of wives, said to have numbered twenty-seven, he delivered his ultimatum:

My wives have got to do one of two things, either round up their shoulders to endure the afflictions of this world, and live the religion, or they may leave, for I will not have them about me. I will go into heaven alone rather than have scratching and fighting around me.[12]

Next, he counseled the other men present on how to handle their wives. He told them to say:

If you stay with me you shall comply with the law of God, and that too without any murmuring and whining. You must fulfill the law of God in every respect, and walk up to the mark without any grunting.[13]

Brother Brigham also said it had been his observation that "Many have been, what shall I say, pardon me, brethren, hen-pecked so much that they do not know the place of either man or woman." The father, he reminded the Saints, was to be master of his own household, and "let the wives and children say 'Amen' to what he says and be subject to his dictates, instead of their dictating the man, instead of their trying to govern him."[14]

161

The obvious disparity between the public defense and the actual practice of polygamy notwithstanding, the Mormons continued waging their vigorous verbal battle to improve their image and preserve their marriage system, but they were not convincing in the least in their efforts to gain the approval of the Gentiles. Hence, after slavery was abolished during the Civil War (1862), many defenders of the national morality moved forward in their campaign to eliminate polygamy, the second "relic of barbarism" they had committed themselves to destroy.

Eastern critics, ignoring the Mormon feminist arguments, still insisted that polygamy was imposed upon the women of Utah. They were convinced that no woman would enter into polygamy of her own free will. As a solution for helping them out of their predicament, an editorial in the *New York Times* in 1867 proposed that suffrage be tried in Utah Territory. Shortly thereafter, a movement toward such a law was underway in the United States Congress. Edward Tullidge, in *History of Salt Lake City*, gives an account of the proceedings:

Mr. (George W.) Julian, delegate from Indiana, offered a bill to the House in 1867 which was "a bill to solve the polygamic problem" by giving women of Utah Territory the power to break up the institution of polygamy and emancipate themselves from the sponsored serfdom and degradation.[15]

After the presentation of the bill, Utah's delegate,

William Hooper, reportedly called upon Mr. Julian and engaged in the following conversation: "Mr. Julian," he said, "that bill has a high-sounding title. What are its provisions?" Julian replied, "Simply a bill of one section providing for the enfranchisement of the women of Utah." To that Hooper replied, "Mr. Julian, I am in favor of that bill." Asked by Julian if he spoke for the leading men of Utah, Hooper allowed that he did not but he said, "I know of no reason why they should not also approve it."[16]

Upon returning to Utah, Hooper met with Brigham Young to discuss the bill. Since they were not threatened by such a bill in any way, the Mormon authorities agreed they should favor it. "No more was said," writes Tullidge, "but from that time the subject seemed to develop itself in the mind of the President (Young), and soon afterward it was taken up by the Utah Legislative body (composed of Mormon leaders) and passed by unanimous vote."[17] With the passage of that first suffrage bill went the stipulation that women would be ineligible to hold high judicial, legislative, or executive offices, though "they might be allowed to hold minor positions." Explaining the conditions in the *Ogden Junction*, Franklin D. Richards wrote:

Mormonism seeks to provide for, educate and make useful to the state, the whole feminine portion of the race. However, women ought not be raised above the level of man to be his governor, guide or law-giver, or invested with powers for which nature has not fitted her.[18]

163

The bill for women's suffrage in Utah Territory then, while it was under consideration by the United States Congress, was passed by Utah Territory itself. Actually the passing of the suffrage bill in Mormondom was not altogether surprising since Mormon women had always enjoyed religious franchise and from the beginning had worked cooperatively with men for the survival of the Church. But the *Salt Lake Tribune*, which was an anti-Mormon newspaper at that time, reflected Utah Gentiles' suspicious opinions when it called the bill "a shrewd move on the part of the priesthood to increase the Mormon electorate." Wives represented so many "bought votes," it charged. It was also claimed that Brigham Young had said, "Remember Brother Hooper, anything for statehood," which suggests another reason for his rapid acceptance of the idea. On this issue Young was no doubt motivated by a variety of considerations, but posterity can rest assured that this was not simply an altruistic act for the benefit of the women in the Mormon society.

It is unlikely that the women of Utah would have promoted suffrage for themselves at that time, nor is there any evidence that they took any significant part in its passage. The vote was simply given to the sisters by the male priesthood leaders. Therefore, Mormon women could hardly have been considered suffragists in 1870. They were grateful for the privilege of voting, however, and some of the prominent members expressed their feeling on the subject in the general Relief Society meeting that was held on February 19, 1870, just seven days after the bill was passed. Mrs. Phoebe Woodruff said she was thankful for the privilege that had been granted to women, but she thought they must act in wisdom and not go too fast.

Now that God has moved upon our brethren to grant us the right to female suffrage, let us lay it by, and wait till the time comes to use it, and not run headlong and abuse the privilege.[19]

Following her remarks, Mrs. Prescindia Kimball said, "I am glad to see our daughters elevated with man and the time come when our votes will assist our leaders and redeem ourselves." Mrs. Zina D. Young mentioned how grateful she was for the privilege of associating with kings and priests of God. Next Sister M.T. Smoot spoke of their great work in Mormonism and of the principles they had embraced which were a salvation to them. But Mrs. Smoot warned:

Many principles are advanced in which we are slow to act. There are more to be advanced. Women's rights have been spoken of. I have never had any desire for more rights than I have. I have considered politics aside from the sphere of woman; but as things progress, I feel it is right that we should vote, though the path may be fraught with difficulty.[20]

It was not surprising to discover, however, that a

few of the women in this complex society had been harboring some genuinely feminist ideas which began to surface at this meeting. Mrs. Wilmarth East, while expressing her feeling that "obedience is better than sacrifice" and that she desired "to be on the safe side and sustain those above us," said nevertheless:

I cannot agree with Sister Smoot in regard to women's rights. I have never felt that woman had her privileges. I always wanted a voice in the politics of the nation, as well as to rear a family.[21]

The even more radical Sarah Kimball took the opportunity to say, "I have waited patiently a long time, and now that we are granted the right of suffrage, I shall openly declare myself a woman's rights woman. She called upon those who would do so to back her up, "whereupon many manifested their approval." Mrs. Kimball, who explained that she had moved in all grades of society, had been both rich and poor, and had always seen much good and intelligence in women, admitted to the sisters:

I have entertained ideas that appear wild, which I think would yet be considered women's rights. Women will have as much prejudice to overcome in occupying certain positions as men will in granting them.[22]

Yet even Sister Kimball conceded in the conclusion

of her bold feminist declaration that "woman is the helpmate of man in every department of life."

The Relief Society members devoted the entire meeting to the new privilege that had come to them instead of following their previously planned agenda, and from that point on they became committed to the suffrage principle. However, since Mormon women were committed to the polygamy principle as well, they, of course, never used the vote to "free themselves" from it, which confused and disappointed their Eastern critics and sympathizers. Ironically, they used their new political power instead in their continued efforts to protect their marriage style. And the foes of polygamy, having been foiled in their scheme, soon began looking for ways to have the Utah suffrage law rescinded.

For almost two decades the hostile Gentiles continued their endeavor to outlaw polygamy, now having to cope with the additional aggravation that the "senseless" Mormon women involved had been given the vote. In addition to a series of antipolygamy bills that came before the United States Congress, the complexities of polygamy as they related to Federal law were taken under consideration by the United States Supreme Court in the George Reynolds case of 1878–1879. This case was appealed after Reynolds was twice tried and found guilty of bigamy in Utah Territory by Federally appointed "Gentile" judges who were not sympathetic to Mormon philosophy. Reynolds, functioning as a test case, named his religious beliefs as justification for violating the Federal anti-bigamy act of 1862. It became imperative for the court first to define exactly what was meant by "constitutionally guaranteed freedom of religion in America" before addressing itself to the question at hand: whether religion provided an acceptable reason for acting in defiance of the law. The court interpreted that freedom to mean that interference with religious beliefs and opinions is illegal, but religious practices must be subject to legal restrictions. Otherwise, declared the court, it would be acceptable for religious worship to include such rituals as the offering of human sacrifice. "Doctrines of religion would become superior to the law of the land, and each citizen could become a law unto himself."

Then, in deciding whether religion should be allowed to interfere with marriage laws, the court reviewed English and American common and civil laws and traditions on the subject and concluded that religious practices were not intended to override legislation regarding marriage, "the institution upon which society is said to be based." Finally, after ruling the anti-bigamy act of 1862 constitutional, the Supreme Court determined that Reynolds' religious beliefs did not, in fact, provide a legitimate reason to violate that law. In legally curtailing freedom of religious practices in America, the court prepared the way for the subsequent Congressional actions which ultimately and specifically made the Mormon plural marriage system illegal.[23]

With each new bill against them, the Mormon women, guided by their patriarchal leaders, reacted to the assault upon their women's rights by holding giant "indignation mass meetings," calling forth thousands of the sisterhood on each occasion. In 1878 an anti-polygamy society was formed by Gentiles of Utah which joined in the national campaign. This so disturbed the Mormon women that an estimated 1,500 sisters of the Relief Society rose up in protest in the old Salt Lake Theater. The able Relief Society leaders among them became the pride of the kingdom as they drew up resolutions and united the women in exercising their constitutional right to petition the United States Government. Some of the petitions, in fact, were personally delivered to Washington by the women. The anti-polygamy Cullom Bill, which had been introduced several times before, came before the United States Senate again in 1880, this time revised to include disfranchisement. Possibly because of the influence of the women's actions in their own defense, that bill was defeated once more. All the while these female activists were increasing their political expertise, verbal skills, and organizational ability; developing pride in their contributions to the community; and acquiring a strong self-image. And proportionately, as the Gentile movement to repeal suffrage in Utah grew, the suffrage platform of Mormon women strengthened.

169

It was during this period of time, in June 1872, that some of the leading women launched their remarkable periodical, *Woman's Exponent*. The second publication expressly for women in the western United States, this eight-page, bimonthly subscription journal was woman-managed, -supported and -produced. Although its stated primary purpose was to serve the needs of Relief Society women with both local items and news of national interest, the more ambitious objective of improving Mormon public relations was clearly acknowledged as well. The editors hoped for a wide circulation among the Gentiles, and in the January 1873 issue they wrote:

The women of Utah today occupy a position which attracts the attention of intelligent and thinking men and women everywhere. They have been grossly misrepresented through the press by active enemies who permit no opportunity of appealing to intelligence and candor of fellow countrymen and women in reply. Who are so able to speak for the women of Utah as the women themselves? It is better to represent ourselves than be misrepresented by others.[24]

Indeed, through their newspaper, the Mormon sisters represented themselves very well. Their journalistic examples, which covered a broad variety of subjects, were of respectable literary quality, demonstrating that many of the sisters were both reasonably intelligent and well-educated and that their views were not so different from those of "normal"

170

American women. It was clear that motherhood and the home were of prime importance to them, and in extolling such virtues as charity, modesty, hard work, and obedience to principle, they exuded proper Victorian idealism in every way.

Paradoxically, if their journal portrayed Mormon plural wives as different in any way from the majority of nineteenth-century American women, it was in their enthusiastic advocacy of women's rights. A column was regularly reserved for the specific purpose of espousing suffrage and other women's causes, under the motto "For the rights of the women of Zion, and for the rights of women of all nations." Their women's rights platform called for equal rights in education, politics, and the professional world, and their articles discouraged women from becoming extravagant and useless objects. Echoing the teachings of Brigham Young, the Mormon sisters urged women toward economic self-sufficiency instead.

The extent to which the feminist ideas expressed in the *Exponent* were shared among the women of Mormondom is difficult to ascertain, but the editorial staff and leaders of the Mormon Relief Society, most of whom were multiple wives of church officials, unquestionably became outstanding spokeswomen of the day on behalf of suffrage and women's rights. It is interesting to find that contributing authors, supported in their feminist endeavor, occasionally ventured beyond what would have been a patriarchy-approved platform, venting some surprisingly negative attitudes about women's subordination and male authoritarianism. Nevertheless, the *Exponent* articles never mentioned women as oppressed in polygamy, but instead, consistently portrayed their marriage style as more liberating than monogamy. In advocating their feminist causes, the Mormon sisters never faltered in their support of Church teachings, nor did they question the priesthood authority or the Mormon patriarchal system in any way.

With all their talking and writing, however, the "Mormon feminists" still failed to impress their critics. Non-Mormons, continuing in their efforts to outlaw polygamy and repeal suffrage in Utah, still claimed that if Mormon women would not help themselves, they must be ignorant, immoral, or deluded, or all three, and therefore, could not be fit to vote. Because of the growing non-Mormon population in Utah Territory, a general Gentile/Mormon controversy had also been increasing in intensity. Mr. William Claggett of neighboring Montana had expressed some of the anti-Mormon feelings when he spoke in the United States House of Representatives on January 29, 1873:

My friend from Utah (Delegate Hooper) goes on to say that Utah is a long way in advance of the age in one respect, that female suffrage has been adopted there. What was the reason for adopting that measure? Was it because the peculiar institution of the Territory recognizes in any degree whatever the elevation, purity and sanctity of women? No, sir. When the Union Pacific Railroad was complete and when the influx of miners and other outsiders began to come into the territory, the chiefs of the Mormon hierarchy, fearing that power would pass from their hands by the gradual change of population, by adopting female suffrage trebled their voting power by a stroke of the pen, and I am credibly informed by the authority of at least fifty men that in practice in that territory any child or woman from twelve years old and upwards, that can wear a yard of calico, exercises the prerogatives of a freeman, so far as voting is concerned.[25]

Tullidge noted that a burst of laughter followed the delegate's flippant remark about the Mormon women exercising the prerogatives of freemen, indicative of the widespread suspicion in regard to suffrage among the polygamous Saints.

It is easy to see why the national movement to repeal suffrage in Utah was confusing to Eastern feminists, who were the nation's leading suffragists. They were indeed faced with a strange dilemma. Legitimate feminists of the East had assumed that the Mormon women would use the vote to help themselves out of polygamy, but they realized that taking away their suffrage privilege because it had not been used in the "right way" would represent a step backward for the suffragists' cause. But after debating the problem, perhaps out of disbelief, the New York Suffrage Association decided to petition the United States Congress in 1873 in support of Utah women's suffrage. Still hopeful of the desired outcome, they insisted that "Utah women themselves would be a powerful aid in doing away with the horrible institution of polygamy. Women are the principal sufferers from this cruel custom, and it is unjust to deprive them of a voice in the suppression."[26]

The sisters out in Utah Territory perceived themselves to be among the leaders of the national suffrage movement, but because of their polygamous habits, they were not even invited to send delegates to the National Suffrage Association meetings until 1879. The conservative wing of the organization, headed by Lucy Stone, was reluctant to include them even then, but Susan B. Anthony and Elizabeth Cady Stanton and their liberal faction were inclined to include all who were interested in the cause. While not sympathetic to polygamy, Stanton spoke up in defense of the Mormon group, making this point:

If George Cannon (of Utah) can sit in the Congress of the United States without compromising that body on the question of polygamy, I would think Mormon women might sit on our platform without making us responsible for their religious faith. If, as the husband of four wives, he can be tolerated in the councils of the nation and treated with respect, surely wives of only a fourth part of man should be four times as worthy of tender consideration.[27]

It was partly because of their *Woman's Exponent* that the Mormon suffragists finally gained acceptance to the national suffrage organization. In fact, in

1877, the editors received a letter from its secretary, Virginia Barnhurst of Philadelphia, who told them that in the East Mormon women had been considered "either oriental dolts or domestic drudges," but she assured them their "able little publication would help them provide a better impression of themselves." And, when admittance was finally granted, it was *Exponent* editor Emmeline B. Wells who was chosen along with the fourth wife of Brigham, Zina Young, to travel as delegates to the Washington, D.C., suffrage conference of 1879.

Accepting them as suffragists, if not as polygamists, Stanton and Anthony had been long-time acquaintances of the Mormon suffrage leaders and had shown friendship toward them all along. They had visited in Salt Lake City in June 1871 while touring the western United States on behalf of women's suffrage, and while there, they met with the Mormon women for five hours in the LDS Tabernacle of Salt Lake City. Some years later Stanton recorded her thoughts about that meeting.

As I stood among those simple people, so earnest in making their experiment in religion and social life, and remembered all the persecution they had suffered and all they had accomplished in that desolate, far-off region, where they had indeed made the "wilderness blossom like a rose," I appreciated as never before, the danger of intermeddling with the religious ideas of any people. Their faith finds abundant authority in the Bible, in the example of God's chosen people. When learned ecclesiastics teach the people that they can safely take that book as guide of their lives, they must expect them to follow the letter and the specific teachings that lie on the surface. The ordinary mind does not generalize or see that the same principles of conduct will not do for all periods and latitudes. When women understand that governments and religions are human inventions, that the Bible, prayerbooks, catechisms, and encyclical letters are all emanations from the brain of man, they will no longer be oppressed by the injunctions that come to them with the divine authority of "Thus saith the Lord."[28]

Participation of Mormon delegates in the National Suffrage Association conference likely was viewed by the Saints as a major breakthrough, but it had little effect upon the continuing national opposition to their suffrage and polygamy in Utah Territory. Undaunted in their efforts, the Anti-polygamy Society of Utah convinced the members of Congress in 1886 that they should provide $40,000 for a refuge and rehabilitation center in Utah to shelter polygamous wives who wished to escape their oppression. After two years, the shelter had attracted a total of only four women and had accepted seven men. The shelter was closed in 1893. It provided still another check on reality for the Gentile "do-gooders" who stubbornly refused to see what Stanton had wisely seen from the beginning, that polygamy had come to the sisters with the divine authority of "Thus saith the Lord."

Joseph Smith, the Mormon Prophet, as a general in the Nauvoo
Legion; from a painting by John Hafen (1887).

A visitation of the Angel Moroni to Joseph Smith; from a painting by Lewis A. Ramsey.

Brigham Young in his prime, about 1850.

Eliza R. Snow, plural wife of Joseph Smith and Brigham Young, Relief Society leader, and poet, about 1855.

Patty Sessions (1795–1893), known as the mother of Mormon midwifery, who was said to have assisted with 3,977 births.

Zina D. Young, plural wife of Brigham Young and caretaker of the Mormon silk industry.

Ann Eliza Webb Young, disenchanted polygamous wife and author of *Wife #19: Life in Mormon Bondage.*

Dr. Ellis R. Shipp was the mother of four children and a plural wife when she entered Women's Medical College in Pennsylvania in 1875.

Harper's Weekly portrays Brigham Young admonishing the Saints in the Mormon Tabernacle (1871).

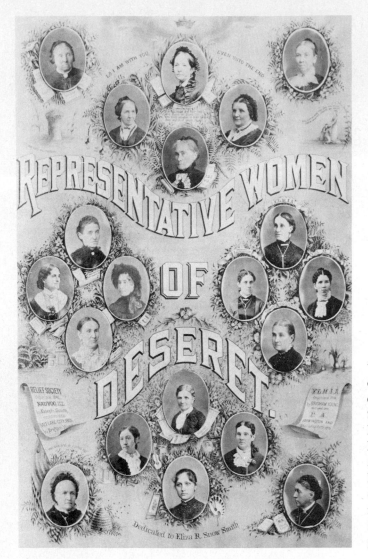

"Representative Women of Deseret," a poster dedicated to Eliza R. Snow Smith, president of the Presiding Board for all Mormon women's organizations (top center). Helen Mar Whitney, who ardently defended polygamy against eastern critics, is at left of left center group.

Mormon life as portrayed in the book *The Mysteries of Mormonism*.

"Waiting for the Old Man." From *The Mysteries of Mormonism.*

Anonymous Mormon cartoon: "Bringing Home a New Wife." Photograph by N.H. Rose.

"The Old Wife and the New." From *The Mysteries of Mormonism.*

The first Mormon Hospital, opened in 1882 in Salt Lake City and operated by the Relief Society.

The Women's Industrial Christian Home in Salt Lake City, a refuge for escaped wives. It attracted only two women and seven men in two years of operation.

The sisters of Zion making silk for the Kingdom, circa 1880.

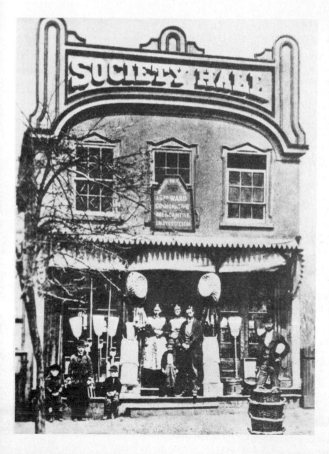

Salt Lake City's 15th Ward Relief Society Hall; Mormon sisters as entrepreneurs.

Emmeline B. Wells, suffragist, editor of *Woman's Exponent*, and Relief Society president, in 1898.

Emily T. Richards, Phoebe Y. Beatie, and Sara M. Kimball, Mormon suffragists.

Brigham Young's daughter Susa as a girl.

Susa Young Gates, suffragist, author, and delegate to the International Council of Women, in 1920.

Dr. Martha Hughes Cannon in 1897, the year after she became the first woman in the United States to be elected to a state legislature.

Brigham Young and nineteen of his twenty-seven wives.

Puck observes the death of Brigham Young (1887).

Brigham Young, Kingdom Builder, in 1876, one year before his death; from a portrait photograph by Charles R. Savage.

Prominent members of the Mormon hierarchy were jailed when polygamy was outlawed in 1887.

The General Board of the Relief Society in 1916.
President Emmeline B. Wells is at front center with book; Susa
Young Gates is second from right, back row.

The St. George Stake Relief Society canning fruit, circa 1930.

Ezra Taft Benson, President, Council of Twelve Apostles.

Belle S. Spafford, president of the Relief Society for thirty years until 1974.

Barbara Smith, president of the Relief Society since 1974.

President Spencer W. Kimball, world leader of the Church of Jesus Christ of Latter-day Saints.

Of course, it is well-known history that in the end the Mormons lost their battle. Following a string of Congressional bills and the Supreme Court decision "to uphold the integrity of marriage," the Edmunds-Tucker Act of 1887 finally succeeded both in making the practice of polygamy illegal under United States law and disfranchising *all* Mormon women and those men who were practicing polygamy. In one last dramatic effort to prevent themselves from being persecuted by their government for their religion, two thousand Mormon women gathered at the Salt Lake Tabernacle in 1886 to demonstrate and petition against a law that threatened to "inflict such grief and indignity upon them," but their resolutions to Congress were to no avail. Despite the vigorous protests, petitions, and sorrowful pleas from the Saints, government officials passed and proceeded to enforce the new law.

Men were temporarily jailed, including the top members of the Mormon hierarchy, church property was confiscated, and families were disbanded, with many wives and children abandoned in the process. It was the women who suffered most when polygamy came to Mormonism, and the women who bore the consequences when it was taken away. Except for underground groups that existed in Utah for several years and families that fled to Canada and Mexico, the sanctioned practice of polygamy ceased among the Mormons. Aware that if they continued to pursue polygamy, they didn't stand a chance for statehood, Mormon Church leaders chose to abide by the law. A few years later, in fact, the Federal law against polygamy was followed by a Church law *prohibiting* polygamy, even though it did not actually refute the principle. The manifesto against plural marriage came from Church President Wilford Woodruff in 1890, and was interpreted generally by the membership as a revelation on the subject. Hence, in one of the greatest religious reversals of all time, the Mormon patriarchy ceased excommunicating members who refused to accept "God's law" of polygamy, and instead, began excommunicating Mormons who continued practicing the law "He" had now rejected.

With the blessings and support of the Mormon leadership, the sisters of the Relief Society remained active as suffragists after polygamy ended. They founded the Woman's Suffragist Association of Utah in 1889, and when the time came to draft a constitution for statehood in 1895, the Mormon suffragists worked diligently to include in it a suffrage law. There was continued strong support for the movement since suffrage leaders were highly respected members of a community where suffrage had worked successfully for seventeen years.

Nevertheless, a heated debate on the suffrage issue took place at the convention in which the constitution was drawn up. This debate, however, had less to do with women's rights per se than with the Mormon-Gentile controversy that was smoldering in

Utah Territory. The real focus of the opposition to women's suffrage then was fear that doubling the Mormon vote would result in the continuing domination of Utah government by the Mormon Church. Records indicate that the votes against suffrage came primarily from non-Mormons, and LDS leader Brigham Roberts, one of the chief orators for the opposition, fell out of favor with the other Church authorities because of his negative stand.

An additional issue in the debate was a genuine concern that a suffrage bill might make the constitution unacceptable to Congress and prevent statehood once again. Nevertheless, the bill was passed by a sizable majority, allowing Utah, upon receiving statehood, to become the third state in the Union to grant women suffrage in its constitution. In that endeavor, the Mormon women were vocal and active participants.

The Mormon Church points with pride to Brigham Young and other early leaders of the Church for their progressive and liberal attitudes toward women in granting them the right of suffrage, a simplistic conception with which many careful historians disagree. As in the economic affairs of the kingdom, evidence of political gain through the effective utilization of women cannot be overlooked as an important motivating force.

In their unique history of political activism, Mormon women never were regarded by others as feminists, but as a result of their religious martyr-

179

dom, they developed into legitimate and enthusiastic suffragists, although they cannot take credit for instituting suffrage in Utah. Typical of Mormonism, suffrage was adopted for the benefit of the institution instead of the individual, and Mormon women were pawns in an institutional political struggle. But the circumstances for its coming to pass notwithstanding, early women's suffrage in Utah has provided justification for the Saints to claim that "Mormon women always have been equal to men."

The equal position of Mormon women as it is related to the Church and hence to the community perhaps was put into proper perspective by Tullidge in *Women of Mormondom:*

> ... it has been said that the women are, equally with their prophets, and apostles, the founders of their church and the pillars of its institutions, the difference being only that the man is first in the order and the woman is his helpmate, or more perfectly said, "they twain are one," in the broadest and most exalted sense.[29]

Thus, Mormondom remains—a land in which, like the Orwellian *Animal Farm*, all are created equal, but some more equal than others. It was with that philosophy that the Saints approached the question of the Equal Rights Amendment in the 1970s.

A transvaluation of values can only be ac-
complished when there is a tension of new
needs, and a new set of needy people who feel
all old values as painful—although they are
not conscious of what is wrong.

Friedrich Nietzsche

7

THE HOTDOG
INVASION

The Equal Rights Amendment to the Constitution
of the United States had met with resistance for fifty
years before it was passed by the United States
Congress in March 1972, subject to ratification by the
states. Therefore, while it passed by a handsome
margin in the Congress and its ratification was accomplished readily by thirty-three of the thirty-eight
states required to make it law, it is not altogether
surprising that the amendment encountered some
difficulty in its final stages. In Utah, where the Mor-

mons maintain pride in their historically progressive tradition regarding women, the ratification of the amendment was soundly defeated each time it was introduced in the legislature. Ironically, the Mormon Church, that valiant defender of suffrage for women, was instrumental in defeating the Equal Rights bill.

Utah was certainly not the only state in which the Amendment failed to pass, and the Mormon Church was not the only church in the country to oppose the idea, but the manner in which the ERA was defeated in Utah raised some interesting political issues. What seemed to be a paradoxical situation angered and confused many who were under the impression that it would have been in keeping with Utah and Mormon tradition to be among the first to endorse the Amendment.

The Utah equal rights proponents first began to organize in the fall of 1972, anticipating the bill's introduction in the 1973 legislative session. A subcommittee of the Governor's Committee on the Status of Women was appointed to study the bill and serve as a steering committee for the campaign. Proponents were reasonably confident because a Salt Lake newspaper, *Deseret News,* had conducted a poll of the candidates for the legislature that indicated the majority of candidates of both parties were sympathetic to the Equal Rights Amendment.

But as they proceeded in a low-keyed, unsuspecting manner, they began to hear of anti-ERA arguments around the state that carried warnings of the disastrous effects upon society that would result from the Amendment. While proponents responded by establishing a speaker's bureau to explain the ERA and to address themselves to the arguments, it was soon seen that much more than a speaker's bureau was needed to cope with these opposing forces. These forces gathered momentum at such a rapid rate that within a short period their emotionally charged campaign had created an atmosphere of hysteria about the issue which characterized the ERA campaign in Utah until the end.

The opposition movement was organized under the name of Humanitarians Opposed to the Degradation of Our Girls (HOTDOGS). Originating in southern Utah, the group was organized and so named, according to its chairperson, Reba Lazenby, because "in proposing this amendment, the Federal Government had promised every woman in America a T-bone steak, but in effect all that they were getting was a hot dog, and a spoiled one at that."[1] Unlike the ERA proponents of Utah, with their calm, academic approach, the HOTDOGS conducted an aggressive and in many ways more politically sophisticated campaign. So effective were the campaign techniques of the HOTDOGS, in fact, that by the time the ERA came up for consideration in the 1973 legislature it clearly didn't stand a chance of succeeding.

Disappointed ERA enthusiasts were highly critical of the proponent leadership for failing to match the zeal of the HOTDOGS. The committee admitted to being caught off guard and unprepared to deal with the kind of opposition that arose. Since an ineffective campaign contributed to the defeat of the Equal Rights Amendment in 1973, it is important in the late 1970s for citizens to take a closer look at both that campaign and the nature of the opposition to fully understand the interesting situation that developed in Utah.

The radical arguments of the anti-ERA group had the familiar ring of the John Birch Society, causing many to suspect that the HOTDOG organization was a front for the Society. These suspicions were later confirmed in the April 1973 issue of the John Birch magazine *American Opinion,* where HOTDOG leaders were identified as members and praised for carrying out their project effectively. Of course, it is well known that the Birch Society has been the force behind much of the organized opposition to the ERA throughout the country, but in Utah it was observed that the HOTDOGS of the John Birch Society were drawn primarily from the Relief Society of the Mormon Church.

The John Birch Society, and organization committed to combat what it believes to be a threatening internal Communist conspiracy in this country, has strived militantly to maintain the status quo since its founding in 1959. Such movements as civil rights, land-use planning, and the Equal Rights Amendment are considered by them endeavors to bring the United States closer to the Communist state. HOT-

DOG chairperson Reba Lazenby, when privately questioned, said, "American women are being pushed to follow the same pattern as those in Russia and China," and she suggested that governors' committees on the status of women which had supported the ERA in many states besides Utah "have been established by Communists to work for the amendment at the taxpayers' expense."[2]

This Birch Society message also was clearly stated in the literature of one of their California organizations, Happiness of Womanhood:

Women in the United States are being conned into "demanding" the conditions FORCED UPON THEM in the Communist countries. The ultimate maneuver to bring about the complete breakdown of family life had begun under the appealing name of the Women's Liberation Movement. . . .they are drawing in support from thousands of misguided women and even men who do not know that this is all part of the Communist plan.[3]

While the Communist theme was reflected in the outpouring of letters from the Utah HOTDOGS to the legislators, to the press, and to thousands of private citizens, it is not surprising that the main thrust of the anti-ERA campaign in Utah focused upon the threat of destruction of the family as the basic unit of society. The HOTDOGS adapted and circulated the literature of the Illinois housewife Phyllis Schlafly, who, as a national leader of the anti-ERA forces, equates the ERA with "deadly poison masquerading as women's lib." Describing what she considers an assault on American women, Schlafly said:

Women's libbers are trying to make wives and mothers feel unhappy with their career, make them feel that they are second-class citizens and "object slaves." Women's libbers are promoting free sex instead of the "slavery of marriage." They are promoting Federal daycare centers for babies instead of homes. They are promoting abortions instead of families. . . .Let's not permit this tiny minority to degrade the role that most women prefer. Let's not let these women's libbers deprive wives and mothers of the rights we now have.[4]

With the family unit, both temporal and eternal, at the very heart of Mormon philosophy, and the kingdom's current emphasis upon keeping women at home, Schlafly's rhetoric as espoused by the HOTDOGS was particularly influential in Mormon country. Realizing a potential threat to their Mormon institutions as well as to their sacred patriarchal family structure, with its doctrinal obligation to produce large families, Church authorities already had been provoked into regularly reinforcing the Church stand against birth control and abortion and speaking out against the women's movement in general, as we have noted throughout this book. Thus, Birch-inspired HOTDOG arguments against the ERA quickly and easily infiltrated the whole of Mormon society.

It also must be repeated that the HOTDOGS were

cultivating "fertile political ground" with their ultra-conservative philosophy. It has been pointed out that Mormon Church leaders have been associated increasingly with the conservative wing of the Republican Party, their trend toward traditional theological literalism having made them naturally predisposed in that direction. However, because of early problems with the separation of church and state which, along with polygamy, prevented Utah from achieving statehood for forty-seven years, there is a separation of church and state clause in the Utah Constitution which makes Mormon leaders reluctant to interfere directly in political affairs.

Many Gentiles complain that the Mormon population of over 60 per cent dominates the affairs of the state, but it would be both inaccurate and unfair to suggest that conservative Mormons have controlled the vote in Utah over the years. Political trends in Utah, though of conservative shading, generally have followed national patterns. In fact, as Thomas O'Dea observed in *The Mormons,* published in 1957, "The church leadership often points with pride to the fact that it does not control the vote, an interesting reaction conditioned by generations of Gentile resentment and suspicion on this score."[5] It is true, however, that when an issue has moral overtones or is interpreted as being threatening to the institutions of Mormonism, the Church leadership, if not by direct interference, manages to influence its membership from behind the scenes. Such was the

187

case with the "liquor by the drink" issue of the 1960s, for example.

In any case, it is safe to say that many Mormons, adapting the philosophy of and taking counsel from the Church authorities, are comfortable with right-wing politics, a condition that prompted John Birch Society founder Robert Welch to remark in 1966 that "the LDS Church is very good recruiting ground to go to." In fact, it is common knowledge that Elder Ezra Taft Benson, President of the Council of Twelve and next in line to succeed Spencer Kimball as President of the Mormon Church, has been linked with the Birch Society for many years. A spokesperson for that organization stated in 1976 that Elder Benson, because of his position in the Church, does not actually belong to the Society at the present time but "he is one of our biggest promoters, and he blesses us for belonging." Elder Benson's son, Reed, served on the national council of the Birch Society for several years in the 1960s and now has been "called" to serve as a Mormon mission president in the eastern states.

Considering both the extraordinary zeal with which Birch Society members pursue their objectives and the irrepressible proselytizing urge of the Mormons, there has been much speculation about whether the above mentioned and other known Birch connections in the Church can continue to exercise the appropriate restraint in affairs of the state. Certainly the direction of the anti-ERA campaign in

Utah intensified that concern. It is understatement to note that the more liberal members of the Church as well as non-members find it disconcerting to anticipate having someone so closely connected with the Birch Society serving as "prophet, seer and revelator" for four million Mormons.

Because of its compatible atmosphere, Salt Lake City was selected as the site for the Birch-supported American Party national presidential nominating convention in 1976. "It is an ideal place," according to the party's executive director, Earl Jeppson, who went on to say:

... If you want to know what's wrong with America, go to Washington because that's where it's at. If anybody wants to know what's right about America, they ought to come to Utah.... There is a "particular situation" in Utah because there is a spirit here that exists nowhere else in the world. That spirit must go out from here to the rest of the country.[6]

Among those who comprehend the enormous wealth and power of the Mormon Church, many are convinced that the "spirit" of which the American Party leader speaks will, in fact, go out from Utah to the rest of the country. And because that spirit encompasses a rigid and traditional position regarding women's roles, the women's movement in America and its ERA proponents can count the Mormon Church alongside the John Birch Society among its strongest foes.

189

In fact, in an evaluation of the 1973 ERA campaign in Utah in *Society Magazine* in 1974, Margaret I. Miller and Helene Linker, both of Stanford University Law School, suggested what they considered "remarkable parallels" between the Mormon Church and the John Birch Society. Not only do the two groups share a conservative philosophy, but these additional similarities were noted:

First, both the Birch Society and the Mormon Church are fervently patriotic. It is the Mormon belief that the Constitution of the United States was divinely inspired.

Second, they are similarly structured authoritarian organizations. The men at the top of both groups have like backgrounds, being mostly businessmen, often self-made, and are uniformly middle-aged to elderly. The authority comes from the top in each case, but both groups rely heavily upon the volunteer efforts of their members for effective functioning, making considerable demands on the time and energy of their members. The flurry of Church-related activities in which a "good" Mormon participates already has been described, and a similar cooperative group effort is required of loyal Birch Society members.

Third, the authors observed a sense of persecution for a righteous cause in both the Mormons and Birchers. With the belief that they are God's chosen people, selected to establish God's kingdom on earth, the Mormons' cause remains ever clear. In pursuing their goal, they experienced real persecution by the Gentiles in the nineteenth century and that served to reinforce their "theological sense of specialness." By maintaining certain customs peculiar to Mormonism such as the wearing of garments (a special kind of underwear) and practicing taboos against alcohol, tobacco, and caffeine, the Saints continue to be in a separate and often defensive position.

Because the Birch stance of fighting an assumed "Communist conspiracy" is regarded by many as radical, the Society also thinks of itself as persecuted. That the two groups share this feeling was acknowledged by Elder Benson of the Mormon Church in a speech in 1966. He said, "Because of the amazingly effective propaganda against them, it has been very unpopular to defend the Birch Society. I can remember when it was unpopular to defend my own church."[7]

There is no question that Birch Society branches are solidly established throughout the state of Utah, especially in rural areas, but it is difficult to ascertain how many Mormons actually belong to the Society. In spite of their many compatibilities, it is believed that the percentage of Mormons who are actual Birch members is small. However, affiliation with the John Birch Society is irrelevant when it is possible for Mormon leaders, using their own organization, to mobilize an army of Saints into action on behalf of the same right-wing causes. Whether originally inspired by the Birch Society or the Mormon Church,

191

the organizational advantage of the HOTDOGS in the 1973 ERA campaign in Utah was apparent.

Using political tactics outlined in the *Blue Book of the Birch Society*, their guide for "fighting the enemy," the HOTDOGS circulated petitions and conducted a massive letter-writing campaign. Among the voluminous assortment of messages received by legislators, one form letter warned that "those who have succumbed to the rantings and false propaganda of the Equal Rights Amendment will feel the vengeance of a just God upon themselves. . . .Needless to say, if reinforcement for the perversions of the ERA is traceable to your hand, you may be doing more to promote the DOWNFALL OF AMERICA than any other single act of your life!"

Literally hundreds of letters poured into the office of the Governor of Utah from the fervent workers, remarkably similar in content, demonstrating not only the organizational effort, but a most thorough incorporation of Birch arguments with Mormon thought. Many letters spoke, of course, of the Mormon respect for womanhood and of woman's God-created role as mother and helpmate. Typical of Birch Society literature, the majority of writers also expressed concern about women being drafted and showed a bizarre preoccupation with restroom facilities.

ERA's threat to the "divinely inspired Constitution" which would "oppress American women like those of Russia and China" was a recurring theme, nearly always linked with the erroneous assumption that the ERA would eliminate freedom of choice for women to control their own lives. Many such letters then proceeded to explain what "the Church stands for" and some were signed with both names and Church titles such as "Relief Society President" or "Primary President." The following are typical examples from the extensive file of letters possessed by the Governor's Committee on the Status of Women, indicating the extent to which Birch Society and Mormon philosophies were merged:

Dear Governor:
God put women on earth to be a helpmate. You are a Mormon. You know the church standing on sex and morality. Do they put boys and girls using the same restrooms or sleeping quarters? Do you propose to sterilize all women so we can be like men? Men can't give birth and bring spirits into the world. Our women would be like women in China and Russia. We will see our government collapse from Communists in our own country.[8]

Dear Governor:
I feel it is against the tenents of the Church to draft women. . . . And furthermore, in regard to Women's Lib on the subject of men sharing the same lavatory facilities, we think this is absolutely disgusting. As an active member of the Church, I am opposed to the ERA.[9]

Some letters expressed fear of what the ERA might do to the Church itself:

193

... It would turn Church programs into chaos. We would have women passing the sacrament and men learning how to decorate cakes. There wouldn't be any Relief Society or the Priesthood, and you can imagine the problems this would create in the temple. Men and women couldn't set (sic) on separate sides or dress in separate areas.[10]

Four Utah high schools submitted to the governor between sixty and seventy-five girls' signatures on separate anti-ERA petitions, combining HOTDOG literature with their Mormon teachings, and similar group-signed petitions came from groups all over the state, particularly the southern part. That this "plan of Satan" was all a part of the Women's Liberation Movement was pronounced in the entirety of this letter signed "A Latter-day Saint":

Dear Governor:
I would like you to know how ashamed I am of this women's lib.[11]

Opinions expressed in these letters, even when signed with Church titles, represented individuals speaking for themselves and not for the Church. While it was no secret that the Church leadership opposed the women's movement in general, Mormon Church leaders managed to refrain from taking an *official* position on the ERA in 1973.

As expected, *Deseret News*, the Church-owned newspaper, editorialized against the Amendment. The *Salt Lake Tribune*'s opposition came as a surprise, however. The *Tribune* presented the conservative but rational argument that women could be adequately protected under existing laws, expressing confidence in the Supreme Court and local courts to bring about justice. While the HOTDOGS no doubt were elated by the *Tribune*'s stand against the ERA, Birchers likely would not agree that the courts were trustworthy, being convinced the judicial system is infiltrated with Communists.

Such valid ERA-connected issues as protective labor legislation, of major importance in more industrialized states, received little attention in Utah. With their conservative philosophy and deep-seated belief in self-reliance, Mormons generally have been less concerned with protective labor legislation than with the opposing principles of "freedom to contract" and "right to work" laws which enable employees to work without joining a union.

Being perpetually interested in avoiding Federal legislation whenever possible, some of the legislators adopted the popular "states' rights" argument against the ERA. However, on the day of the Utah House's vote on ratification of the ERA, the majority of legislators abandoned such arguments and preferred instead to take up the sentimental theme of woman's God-given roles, specifically defining them according to "revealed" Mormon doctrine.

Arguments about the "natural" differences between men and women that Phyllis Schlafly had spoken of were *naturally* appealing to Mormon legislators. "If you don't like these fundamental differences (that women have babies and men don't), you will have to take up your complaint with God because He created us this way." And stemming from the campaign emphasis upon women's "proper roles," the dramatization and idealization of desirable feminine qualities embellished the House debate. Reflecting the current attitudes of the Mormon leadership, legislators laced their floor speeches with biblical quotations which would verify that women's place is in the home.

On January 24, 1973, the ERA ratification bill failed in the Utah State Legislature by a two-to-one margin. The gallery was packed with uncontrolled demonstrators creating a less than dignified environment. The demonstrators were identified as Mormon Relief Society members who were also there as HOTDOGS. The degree of distortion of the meaning of a bill that simply asked for equal rights under the law was appalling to the ERA proponents, and the caliber of the Utah debates on the subject was deplorable to many, both for and against the amendment.

For many of the Mormon ERA advocates, it was the debunking of a myth. Coming face to face with reality, they realized that Mormon policies toward women were not so progressive after all. And with considerable indignation, some said their grandmothers and great grandmothers who had been stalwarts of the Relief Society and among the most outspoken women's rights leaders in America would have "turned over in their graves" at the anti-feminist display. But would those nineteenth-century Mormon suffragists, in fact, have continued their courageous fight for women's rights had their endeavor not been endorsed by the patriarchy at the time?

In order to get on with our business, we have found it necessary first to exorcise this patriarchal demon from our midst.

Sheila Collins

8

SHE IS MY PRINCESS

As they rose from the dust of defeat in 1973, the Latter-day Saint proponents of equal rights sought to verify that advocacy of women's rights had been a Mormon tradition. They went directly to historical documents where an abundance of evidence was available. In their new campaign literature they proudly informed the Utah public:

Brigham Young was our great and forward-thinking leader. He believed that women were useful not only to keep house and raise babies, but in the fields of business, law, and physics as well. He said, "In following these things, women but answer the design of their creation."[1]

198

Composed primarily of well-educated women, a growing collection of Mormon ERA enthusiasts included one seventy-five-year-old woman who had worked for an equal rights amendment since the passage of the national suffrage bill in 1920. Disturbed by the direction her Church had taken, she reminded the Mormon sisterhood in her printed plea for ratification of the ERA that such Mormon historical favorites as Susa Young Gates, daughter of Brigham Young, Emmeline B. Wells, Emily Tanner Richards, and "any number of prominent LDS women gave lectures all over America on the suffrage platform." This devout Mormon woman, along with many others, viewed her efforts on behalf of the ERA as a natural continuation of the Mormon suffrage endeavor. The Equal Rights Amendment was considered by them entirely compatible with Mormon philosophy as they perceive it, and the "strong woman" image part of their Mormon cultural myth.

Therefore, while the majority of Mormon women continued to accept the argument that the ERA would cause the destruction of the family unit, associating it with the "sinister" women's liberation movement against which current Church leaders warned, a significant number of Mormons with a strong sense of their "feminist" heritage were among the joiners and active participants in a new ERA Coalition for a second attempt at ratification.

With resolve to learn from previous mistakes, the Coalition, supported by thirty-two Salt Lake City women's groups, planned its strategy, concentrating on an extensive reorientation program. Considering the spectacular failure of 1973, the outlook for success was not bright. However, it improved considerably when the Utah Democratic Party, which readily adopted a pro-ERA resolution as part of its platform, won the majority of seats in the House of Representatives in the November 1974 election. Coalition members were further elated when the polls consistently presented a head count in the House of Representatives of thirty-four yes votes, thirty-two no votes, and nine undecided.

Nevertheless, the proponents of the ERA felt uneasy. They feared the power of the Mormon Church, which, in the retrospective view of 1974, generally was thought to have been responsible for the 1973 defeat even though the Church leadership never took an official position in that campaign. Relief Society President Belle Spafford, in an Associated Press interview published in August 1974, once again opposed the ERA. Her statements could not be interpreted as Church policy and very likely had little influence upon the legislators, but they were disconcerting to the pro-ERA people because of the widespread assumption that the Relief Society president is the female voice of the male hierarchy. In addition, anti-feminist messages to women from the Church leadership had been increasing at a rapid rate since the 1973 campaign.

According to its chairperson, the ERA Coalition

contemplated sending a small delegation to the Church leadership to explain their interpretation of what the ERA would and would not do, but the idea was abandoned. The best they could have hoped for was continued silence, and because discussing the issue conceivably could have provoked Church leaders into taking a negative stand, they decided against "rocking the boat." President Kimball had been convincing when he stated to the Associated Press in January 1974 that "the traditional policies of the Mormon Church toward women will not change soon."

Of course, the policies of which President Kimball spoke were not the traditional policies to which the Mormon ERA supporters had been referring in their campaign. And this discrepancy had been rapidly emerging as a major subject of interest and debate in Mormondom. As early as 1971, a group of concerned Mormon women in Boston, Massachusetts, collaborated to write about women in the church in *Dialogue,* an independent Mormon journal which has a wide circulation though it is not sponsored by the Church. Suggesting an awareness of the inconsistency in Church policy in regard to women, these writers expressed strong identification with "Mormon feminists" of the nineteenth century, praising their remarkable accomplishments and the diversity of their lives. Naturally, with women's rights becoming an important national issue, other women in the Mormon culture began to examine their positions.

Specific problems raised by the early ERA campaign had stimulated discussions on the subject in Utah to the extent that there had been a mild polarization among Church members. It began to occur to many Mormon women that in the area of women's rights they might have been losing ground in their culture and Church while other women in the country were moving forward.

Continuing to explore the subject of Mormon women, the Boston group, as Mormon Sisters, Inc., published their first quarterly issue of *Exponent II* in July 1974, reaching a circulation of almost two thousand by the end of the first year. Representing a revival of the nineteenth-century Mormon newspaper, *Woman's Exponent,* it attempted to recapture the feminist spirit exuded in that early publication. But since it is published without the sanction of the church leadership and under peril of official condemnation, its feminist messages have been weak indeed when compared to those of the nineteenth-century publication which had the full endorsement of the Church leadership.

Small "sisterhoods," similar to the one in Boston, began forming in other cities where Mormons are concentrated. The highly educated and professional women belonging to a Salt Lake City group described their purpose for organizing as a variety of shared interests, an important one again being their concern about women's roles both in the Mormon Church and in contemporary society. Finding the

202

Relief Society sometimes stifling to the free exchange of ideas, they felt their sisterhood provided that needed dimension in their lives. Most members of these informal sisterhoods whom I interviewed described themselves as feminists and suggested a wide spectrum of ideas regarding accommodation and change that could be accomplished within the institution of Mormonism.

But the majority shared enthusiasm for the ERA, and they found it regrettable that Belle Spafford, then president of their one-million-member Relief Society, had spoken against the Amendment. These capable and articulate modern-day Mormon women's rights advocates were aware that they must be cautious in promoting the ERA among fellow Mormons in the face of the assumed stand of the Church. When they discussed how far they could go in that direction without repercussions from the Church, naming social ostracism or even excommunication as possibilities, their meetings sometimes took on the atmosphere of underground operations. It was apparent, however, that their conflict with the rigid attitudes of the current Church leadership regarding women's issues stemmed not from antagonism but from a deep concern for their Church, and most of them felt compelled to exercise restraint because they wished to remain members in good standing.

When President Spencer Kimball surprised the LDS membership by appointing Barbara Smith to replace Belle Spafford as Relief Society president in

October 1974, hopes rose in the proponent ranks about the possibility, however remote, that the new, younger Relief Society leader would agree with the more "enlightened" segment of the Church and endorse the ERA. Those hopes were quelled soon, however, when Sister Smith gave a much publicized speech in December 1974 strongly opposing the Amendment. She recited the reasons given by Mrs. Spafford for her stand, saying the Amendment was too broad, too vague, and a threat to the family. In addition, Mrs. Smith, also finding support for her position in Mormon history, quoted the Mormon prophet Joseph Smith on the subject of women:

He taught women to live lives of virtue and to be a comfort to their husbands and delight in them, to remain meek—shall we say teachable—to exhort the Church when called upon to do so, and to learn much.[2]

The usual debate then ensued in Mormondom about whether this was Sister Smith's personal feeling or that of the Church authorities. ERA Coalition leaders reported that when one of their LDS members went directly to Mrs. Smith to inquire, the Relief Society leader confided that she, in fact, had been asked by the authorities to give that speech and had been given permission to privately inform Mormons who called that this was the case.[3] Not wishing to let it be known that Church leaders definitely were opposed to the Amendment, the Coalition members vowed to keep that information to themselves, and they were aided in that endeavor. The Church public relations chairman stated, when asked by the press to respond to the subject, that the Relief Society president had expressed her own personal opinion regarding the ERA and that it did not represent Church policy.

Speculation grew in the mid-1970s about whether the Mormon Church would ultimately remain silent or officially oppose the ERA, and tension surrounding the campaign had reached a new high by the time the convening date of the 1975 legislature arrived. Opposition groups were continuously active, but the hysteria that dominated the 1973 campaign was diminishing. While the *Salt Lake Tribune* editorials continued to insist that the ERA was not really necessary, an increasing number of Mormon women, in a surfacing of the "feminist revival" countermovement within the Church, had been stepping forth to say they thought it *was* necessary. This trend, along with continued support from legislators, brought the ERA proponents to the opening of the legislature in 1975 in a mood of optimism.

But on the eve of that opening date, January 11, the Mormon Church made an extraordinary move. An unsigned editorial opposing the ERA appeared in the Church News section of the Mormon-owned *Deseret News* in a column generally reserved for Church policy statements. While it would be difficult for people outside of the Mormon kingdom to comprehend its significance, that editorial, though unsigned, was viewed by the majority of Utahns as having come from the Mormon First Presidency. Thus, the Mormon Church refrained from making an *official* statement, but the Mormon faithful *believed* their current Prophet had spoken. The editorial itself was not powerful, but its effect was powerful indeed. It dealt a shattering blow to the proponents of the ERA. Here is the text of the "editorial":

EQUAL RIGHTS AMENDMENT

On April 18, 1842, Prophet Joseph Smith, following the organization of the Relief Society, declared: "I now turn the key in your (women's) behalf in the name of the Lord. . . And this society shall rejoice, and knowledge and intelligence shall flow down (upon women) from this time henceforth."

With this declaration, when women's organizations were almost non-existent, the Prophet placed the Church in the forefront of those who have taught the dignified and exalted place of women. To this end, Church leaders from those early times have advocated programs to enhance the status of women as daughters of God. They have also actively given encouragement and support to legislative measures designed to safeguard the welfare of women, the home and the family. Over a period of many decades, women have been accorded special protection and the status properly due them. More recently, these include equality of opportunity in political, civil and economic spheres. BUT NOW THERE ARE many who feel that the way to take care of inequities that may have existed in the past, or may presently exist, is to ratify the Equal Rights Amendment to the Constitution. Legislators in a number of states will be faced with decisions on this question in the next few weeks.

Both Mrs. Belle S. Spafford, recently retired president of the nearly one-million member world-wide Relief Society of the Church, and her successor, Mrs. Barbara B. Smith, have spoken forth-rightly on this question, the former in a widely published interview with George W. Cornell, religion editor of the Associated Press; the latter in a recent talk before the University of Utah Institute of Religion. Among their statements were these:

"It appears that the Equal Rights Amendment is not only imperfect but dangerous."

"The blanket approach of the Equal Rights Amendment is a confused step backward in time instead of a clear stride in the future."

"The Equal Rights Amendment is not the way. It . . . will not fulfill their hopes, but rather would work to the disadvantage of both women and men."

"It is so broad that it is inadequate, inflexible and vague; so all-encompassing that it is non-definitive."

LEGISLATIVE HEARINGS and debate will doubtless produce millions of words uttered on both sides with much emotion. But all of this will not change the fact that men and women are different, made so by a Divine Creator. Each

207

has his or her role. One is incomplete without the other. Out of innate wisdom and the experience of centuries, lawmakers have enacted measures for the benefit and protection of each of the sexes but more particularly for women. In this country they have already provided statutory equality of opportunity in political, civil and economic affairs. If this has not always been extended, it has usually been the result of enforcement rather than absence of law.

Overnight the yes votes in the House of Representatives plummeted from thirty-four to sixteen as indicated in an official poll, the defections obviously resulting from the editorial. Emphasizing the fact that the editorial was unsigned, some legislators questioned the widespread assumption that the Mormon Prophet, in fact, had spoken and were prompted to go directly to the Church offices to consult the Mormon leadership. Included in that group were the six women legislators sponsoring the new ERA bill and two male representatives, one of whom had been its co-sponsor in 1973. The legislators were unable to see the Church President or his counselors, but they spoke to an assistant who verified that the Church was opposed to the ERA. He reminded them, however, that as Mormons they had the right to their "free agency" of course and that each should vote his own conscience. They also were reassured that there would be no church reprisals—no bishops serving in the legislature would be removed from office for vot-

ing affirmatively on the Amendment. The courageous women legislators in the group, all members of
the Mormon Church, declared they would remain
firm in their commitment to the ERA, but both of the
men who had been committed "yes" votes defected,
one with a statement that was quoted in the *Salt Lake
Tribune* the following day: "It is my Church (LDS),
and as a bishop, I'm not going to vote against its
wishes."[4]

An outburst of public criticism from Gentiles and
liberal Mormons alike flooded the media in response
to an elected representative making such a statement.
Many writers both for and against the ERA expressed
outrage at his allegiance to the Church instead of to
his constituency, terming his action "a flagrant viola-
tion of the separation of church and state principle."
Ultimately, after a poll conducted in his district indicated that his constituency was almost evenly
divided on the ERA issue, this bishop-legislator
agreed to vote for the amendment as he had originally promised "if the vote is not close."

The ERA Coalition itself experienced some defection of LDS members following the Church editorial,
but in the long run, the editorial had the effect of
strengthening Coalition support. Unsolicited donations were sent along with offers of help from people
who were reacting to the display of power by the
Mormon Church.

The fact that the Church had spoken without actually taking an official stand became a sensitive issue

among ERA proponents. Many felt that, having gained control over the ERA in Utah, Church leaders should admit to having taken an official position. On the other hand, if the Mormon Church wished to avoid the stigma of an official statement, members, particularly legislators, shouldn't have been influenced to such an extent. Therefore, the ERA Coalition leaders decided upon sending a letter by registered mail to the Church President to ascertain how the editorial should be viewed, declaring their intentions to publicize the editorial nationally as an official statement unless otherwise informed.

After waiting an appropriate length of time for a response, Coalition leaders called a press conference to charge that the fate of the ERA in Utah to that point was being determined by the LDS Church rather than the state legislature. Asked to interpret the editorial from his point of view, an invited dignitary from the Mormon Church stated that only the First Presidency of the Church can speak officially for the Church, and therefore, he did not view the *Deseret News* editorial as doctrine. "There are Mormons for and Mormons against the ERA," he continued, "and each must use his free agency, including the legislators." He then commented, "The Church is careful not to get mixed up in politics directly," which drew hearty laughter from the crowd at the conference.

More than a month passed before a one-line reply from the Mormon Church leadership came to the leaders of the Coalition. It said, "We have received and noted your letter in relation to the ERA." In the meantime, the Associated Press and United Press International had been notified that the LDS Church had opposed the ERA.

As explained in Chapter 3, according to Mormon theology the gift of "free agency" is the freedom given to human beings to choose good over evil and thus gain eternal salvation by merit. However, that term is bandied about quite carelessly in Mormonism. When used in regard to such issues as the ERA, as suggested by the Church leaders, is free agency properly exercised to support the Church point of view because it is "good," and if so should it be concluded that supporting the ERA would be "evil"? There is evidence to suggest that a subtle coercion is involved in the use of this term. This was demonstrated when an assistant professor at Brigham Young University, an articulate proponent of the ERA who had been scheduled to speak to legislators' wives during the opening week of the legislative session, found herself in a position of publicly taking issue with the Church authorities. It was thought to be at great personal risk that she used her "free agency" and proceeded with her pro-ERA speech in view of the Church editorial. But nevertheless she held forth, explaining,

I am aware of those who would exercise unrighteous dominion, those who are manipulators, social engineers,

211

and those who would use compulsion and church positions to demand adherence to their political persuasion.

A devout Mormon, this individual expressed her view that the ERA was an additional inspiration to the Constitution, and lamented that the most unfortunate aspect of the whole issue had been the polarization between factions within the Church and the state.

That her position was somewhat tenuous as a result of her "free agency" performance was apparent. An article appeared in the *Salt Lake Tribune* the following week suggesting there had been considerable speculation about retaliation from the church-owned Brigham Young University. Captioned WON'T LOSE JOB, SAVANT SAYS OF ERA, the article quoted the woman as saying, "I'm not going to be excommunicated from the Church, and my job is not in jeopardy as things now stand." She acknowledged that there had been two conferences with the university president, but she said, "We simply discussed my position on the ERA, and he was concerned about what might happen to me in terms of how others might judge me."[5] Whether she was judged harshly by church authorities and the University leaders for her continued support of the ERA is not clear, but the following year the savant's contract was not renewed.

Extensive publicity about this Mormon woman

who spoke out so boldly brought the dichotomy on the subject of Mormon women further into public focus. The two factions met head-on in letters to the press, primarily from Mormon women who either criticized her for taking exception to the Church leadership or praised her for her courage in publicly speaking out for women's rights. Some wrote of "the LDS woman's designated roles" and the "position of honor she enjoys in the Church" while others compared this modern LDS feminist to their "sturdy, independent grandmothers" who gave Utah a "position of honor in the fight for women's rights." Specific Mormon ancestors were named along with "great ladies of the Relief Society" who, according to contributors, most assuredly would have supported the Equal Rights Amendment.

With the public so sensitized, introduction of the ERA bill in the legislature was delayed as long as possible by the proponents, not only to gain time in their efforts to recapture lost support, but for the reason stated in the *Salt Lake Tribune* of January 26, 1975: ". . .proponents held off to quell various threats to the projected sponsors' political futures." The Democratic Central Committee not only reaffirmed its pro-ERA platform, but pledged special assistance to potential sponsors to avoid the "political suicide" that might result. Nevertheless, one LDS legislator who had agreed to sponsor the bill not only declined that role, but later voted against the bill as well. In the long run, the time gained for additional campaigning proved an exercise in futility because the proponents failed to garner any of the lost votes.

House Bill HJR20, The Equal Rights Amendment, was debated and voted upon February 19, 1975, in the Utah State Legislature. Because there was no question about the outcome, the debate was but a charade for the benefit of the packed gallery and the overflow crowd seated in the rotunda of the State Capitol. After the bill's introduction by the LDS women legislators, proponent leaders, including some prominent Mormon women, gave their well-prepared arguments with courage and dignity. But, with the exception of a short discussion of the question of state versus Federal legislation of women's rights, the legislators proceeded once again more in the fashion of a religious assembly than a legislative session, giving dramatic presentations about the divine roles of womanhood as set forth in the Bible and Mormon doctrine.

As an inevitable feature of American patriarchal society, religious overtones have been present in legislative debates on women's issues, including the ERA, in every section of the country. But in Utah religious domination had been the underlying concern throughout the campaign. Constantly in need of the reminder, Utah legislators once again were given the essential warning by one of their women colleagues who told them, "We as legislators must uphold the total separation of church and state."

214

However, it was an LDS male legislator who most attracted attention of House observers when, in defense of Mormon progressive traditions regarding women, he pointed out that "a vote against equal rights is not being against equal rights." And as the debate came grinding to a finish, another priesthood-holding representative summed up his anti-ERA dissertation and perhaps the tone of the entire house debate by concluding, "I love my wife. She is my princess." Audible groans came from the women of the proponent gallery among whom sat the previously mentioned seventy-five-year-old ERA advocate, a devout Mormon and a widow who, having worked to support herself and her children for forty years, no doubt considered herself more in the category of "working woman" than "princess." In fact, the Mormon legislators and the patriarchy seemed to have forgotten that a woman of the Mormon culture traditionally has been a working woman instead of a princess.

In requiring Utah to incorporate a separation of church and state clause in their constitution before granting statehood, the United States Congress had acted wisely. With well over 60 percent Mormon population in the state, many of whom regard Church pronouncements as revelation, the democratic process easily could be abused. Legislators who show first allegiance to the Church leadership definitely raise some questions regarding that principle, ethical, if not legal. But in spite of the protests

215

and shouts of "foul" from those who disagreed with the Mormon authorities, the Church editorial opposing the Equal Rights Amendment did not represent an illegal act on the part of the leadership, nor would such an editorial, signed or unsigned, actually violate the separation of church and state principle. Churches have the same right as other organizations to express a point of view. However, the strategically placed editorial did have the effect of short-circuiting the legislative system and unquestionably defeated the ERA in Utah the second time around. It also revived, once again, the Mormon/non-Mormon controversy in regard to the political scene in the state, and intensified the growing conflict among women of the Church.

When asked to comment on the ERA in my taped interviews, many of the Mormon faithful defended their Church's constitutional right and responsibility to give views on moral issues, which they considered the ERA to be. As expected, others denied that the Church, in fact, had taken a stand because the editorial was unsigned. But a large number of Mormon women again were dismayed by the Church's leadership. While acknowledging that leaders feel duty-bound to protect the way of life for a significant American sub-culture, these women believed the Church interference with the *political issue* of the ERA was unwarranted and that the editorial represented a misuse of power.

"What made me really angry," said one critic, "is

how smart they were politically. They got what they wanted without being tainted."[6] And another, in a charge heard repeatedly since the settling of Utah Territory, said, "It did show the world that the LDS Church calls the shots with regard to politics in this state."[7]

Mormons were by no means "calling the shots" but were vigorously campaigning against the ERA in other states as well, according to reports from the national ERA organization. It was noted in the *Salt Lake Tribune* that Mormon legislators helped defeat the Amendment in Nevada and that the Mormon Church was behind Idaho's attempt in 1976 to rescind the pro-Amendment bill that had been passed there.

In rejecting the ERA, the Mormon Church was joined by several other religious denominations in the country. But the bill was not considered "evil" by the majority of churches in America who, along with many denominations in the state of Utah, actively supported the Amendment. Whether one is for or against the ERA, it is safe to say that no religious organization in America has been more assertive than the Latter-day Saint Church in promoting its point of view. In explaining that point of view, columnist Joan Beck of the *Chicago Tribune* captured its essence when she quoted President Spencer Kimball on the subject: "What woman would want any greater glory or tribute than that which comes from an appreciative and loving husband?"

Of course, the views of the Mormon ERA advocates and their efforts to re-establish Mormon women as leaders in the field of women's rights received little recognition nationwide. But the continuing paradox surrounding the woman question in Mormondom was emphasized again in an interesting vignette that occurred in the spring following the second defeat of the ERA in Utah. Officers of the Salt Lake City chapter of the Utah Women's Political Caucus, in presenting their annual "Susa Young Gates Awards," praised the life of that important woman of Utah history. Describing her as a suffragist of national standing and a women's rights advocate, they compared Susa's contributions to those of the women currently working to elevate the status of women in Utah. And for that reason the Women's Caucus selected as recipients of the 1975 Susa Young Gates awards four women who had made significant contributions to the pro-ERA campaign.

In accepting the awards the women confirmed their beliefs that there always has been and still remains a strong commitment to women's rights among Utahns, which includes a belief in the ratification of the Amendment that had twice failed. One of the award winners, a former legislator, a mother of fifteen, a grandmother of sixty-nine, and a Mormon ward Relief Society president, said she agreed with the Mormon President that homemaking is the greatest role of a woman, but "a homemaker needs the education and training to understand the world around her, and a good marriage is built on love, trust, and equal rights."

There was speculation in the Mormon community that the independent stand of this extraordinary Mormon woman would have an adverse effect upon her status in the Church. In addition, a vigorous protest against all of the awards was heard from the Brigham Young Family Association. The *Salt Lake Tribune* reported that a letter was sent to the chairperson of the sponsoring organization by Mr. Orson Whitney Young on behalf of the Young family complaining that "It is a mockery to the honored name of Susa to present awards in her name to women who took a position on an issue (ERA) contrary to the stand of the leadership of the Church of Jesus Christ of Latter-day Saints."[8] His interpretation was that the Church had taken an unmistakable stand, and he also noted that the present Relief Society president and her predecessor had issued statements opposing the ERA. Young pointed out that Susa had been a member of the Church Relief Society Board, and, listing her many significant contributions to the Church, he concluded, "We therefore earnestly protest you giving these awards in the name of the kinswoman we so much admired."

It is from tales of Mormon women such as Susa Young Gates that modern-day sisters of the Church have developed an identity crisis. Born March 18, 1856, in the historic Lion House where her father,

Brigham, lived with his multitudes of wives, Susa grew up to be a remarkable woman indeed. One of the original Mormon "super-women," this mother of thirteen managed time for an unusual variety of activities outside of the home. It is especially interesting to contemplate the logistics involved in this Utah woman's arranging, before the jet age, three European journeys as a delegate to meetings of the International Council of Women. In fact, Susa served as the sole United States delegate to the Copenhagen meeting of 1901, one of the highest honors for a woman of that time. Representing the YLMIA, she attended seven National Council of Women meetings as well, serving as press chairman of that organization for three years.

However, the well-educated Susa was known best as a prolific writer. "To uplift the youth of her people with her pen" was a mission given her by her father. Therefore, as founder and editor of *The Young Woman's Journal*, she wrote a great deal about spiritual and doctrinal matters. But under the nom de plume of "Homespun," Susa also wrote on a variety of subjects, including suffrage and women's rights, for *Woman's Exponent*. "Determined to go to Harvard University," she spent one summer there studying English, and later wrote several novels and a history of the YLMIA.

Biographies of Susa nevertheless say her "devotion as a wife and mother was her first religious duty, and her obedience to authority and reverence for the

priesthood were the foundation stone of her life.'''[9]
There is intrigue, however, when biographers describe her as a vivid personality with a complex character and artistic temperament, "her emotional nature held in check by the saving grace of honor."[10]
And what the biographers do not describe, in
another case of "carefully laundered" Mormon history, is that Susa's first marriage to Dr. Alma Dunford
lasted five years, produced two children, and ended
in divorce. Dr. Dunford, a dentist in St. George,
Utah, apparently drank heavily, which, along with
Susa being unprepared for married life at age sixteen, caused the marital strife, according to family
survivors.[11] While Dr. Dunford was away serving on
an LDS mission in England in 1877, Susa filed for
divorce. Upon being served notice, Dr. Dunford
"became so infuriated that he came home at once and
is said to have had Susa hailed into Judge Hagen's
court in St. George where she spent one night in
jail."[12]

The divorce was never mentioned publicly by Susa
or the family. A descendant of the family has
suggested that "There must have been behind what
she wrote and did a desire that her young readers
might be spared some of the heartaches of an unsuc-
cessful marriage."[13] It is reported that while the families of the couple couldn't condone Brother Dunford's alcoholism, they considered it unfortunate
that the young wife obtained a divorce while her
husband was abroad. And since the Mormon Church

221

can't condone divorce, they no doubt thought it was unfortunate that Susa obtained a divorce at all. It is interesting that the civil divorce granted in 1877 was not made final in the LDS Temple by Mormon President Wilford Woodruff until 1890, after the death of Brigham Young, even though Susa had remarried in 1880 and Brother Dunford took a new wife in 1882.

Guilt-ridden Mormon divorcees of today can take comfort in knowing that an accurate historical account of this idealized Mormon woman, Susa Young Gates, reveals her to be no less outstanding, but a little more human, and suggests she used her free agency at least some of the time. Whether or not this women's rights advocate would have supported the ERA today against the judgment of the Church leadership is an open question, but in their response to the Young Family Association protest which was published in the *Salt Lake Tribune*, the women of the Political Caucus said that while they could appreciate the family's concern, "they don't have a monopoly on Susa. . . and if she were alive today she would be proud of the women we honor."[14]

That the many ERA-Mormon Church-related incidents had created a controversy in Zion was apparent from what appeared to be an interminable supply of letters to the media. Recurring themes in the postmortem communications were expressed in such statements as "I never dreamed that the great state of Utah, the first to exercise woman's suffrage, would defeat the ERA," and "The Mormon Church of all churches, where women are held in such high esteem, should have aided rather than defeated the ERA."

The letters finally stopped appearing, but the issue was not forgotten. The third annual women's conference presented at the University of Utah in October 1975 attracted a record crowd of nearly four thousand people, young and old, Mormon and non-Mormon. Repercussions from the Mormon-ERA conflict were felt throughout the conference where, in an atmosphere of a "giant pep-rally," many non-Mormons focused repeatedly on the Church hierarchy as a deterrent to women's rights. But this was not the case with the Mormons there. It likely would have been viewed by feminists outside the Mormon kingdom as a curious phenomenon to hear women announce on the microphone, "I'm a Mormon and I'm proud of it, and I'm a feminist, and I'm proud of it." Conference guest Gloria Steinem cheered the crowd on by remarking, "People who say Mormon women are not speaking out for their rights are mistaken," but she later confided to conference leaders that she wondered if it would be possible to be a Mormon and a feminist at the same time.

Feminism suffers from a lack of precise definition. However it may be defined, the point must be emphasized again that feminism can never properly be perceived as compatible with patriarchal religion. But most particularly, it can never be appropriately identified with the Mormon religion, in either its modern-day version or in Mormonism of the past, despite any and all claims to the contrary. In fact, in one additional unique way, as the following chapter will verify, as functional philosophies Mormonism and feminism stand out as diametrically opposed.

Nevertheless, we must recognize that many of the most diligent workers in the ERA campaign in Utah were devout members of the Mormon Church who, in working thus, perpetuated what they consider to be the Mormon feminist tradition. Some Mormon sisters, for better or for worse, have their own brand of feminism which is, in some ways, as out of tune with the mainstream of feminism today as that of the nineteenth-century suffragists who were living in polygamy.

Why should not woman be the second in sequence, but only in sequence? What other choice has she, seeing she can be nothing at all apart from this sequence and her place within it?

Karl Barth

9

UNMARRIED IN A MARRIED CHURCH

There is no more fascinating historical investigation than tracing the development of patriarchies, the root of our sexist society, from early civilizations through the ages to the present time. Today, by conceiving of God as a male and from that assuming the appropriateness of an all-male priesthood and a patriarchal family order, patriarchies cause and perpetuate sexism in varying degrees. However, nowhere in patriarchal history or in present-day practice is there an innovation comparable to the Mormon eter-

225

nal marriage law, and in regard to the status of women, that law separates Mormonism from all other religious organizations.

While the marriage law and its effect upon Mormon life has been explained and repeatedly noted in earlier chapters, often in relation to its claimed advantage to women, the reference here is to its devastating effect upon the single women in the Church, a subject worthy of separate attention. The Latter-day Saint system may command the respect of non-Mormon Americans for placing a high value on the family, but it is important to recognize the single woman as a casualty of that system.

Taking a closer look at the marriage law as it relates to the single woman then, it bears repeating that Mormon marriage goes beyond the patriarchal designs of the Bible by declaring marriage eternal *and* by making eternal salvation in the Celestial Kingdom *contingent* upon marriage. Additionally, with the single woman in mind, it should be re-emphasized that the primary purpose on earth for all men and women of the Church is to marry and produce children. Beyond God's commandment to "replenish the earth," the Saints are obligated to produce children to provide bodies for spirits in the pre-existence waiting to be born.

The consequences resulting from failure to perform these religious duties are specifically outlined in Section 132 of the *Doctrine and Covenants*. The doctrine warns that those without temple marriages will become

angels in heaven, which angels are ministering servants, to minister for those who are worthy of a far more, and an exceeding, and an eternal weight of glory. For these angels did not abide by law; therefore, they cannot be enlarged, but remain separately and singly, without exaltation in their saved condition, to all eternity, and from henceforth are not Gods, but are angels of Gods forever and ever.

It has been pointed out that participation in this essential aspect of Mormon "eternal progression" virtually rules out the possibility of total option in career choice for women, making adherence to both feminist and Mormon principles impossible. For Mormon women, the status of unmarried is considered unfortunate, but the *choice* of unmarried is unacceptable. And while it is possible for a Mormon woman to select a profession in addition to motherhood, to do so *instead* of motherhood is unacceptable. "This is an area," according to a spokesperson of the Church, "where a Latter-day Saint woman would have to struggle with her conscience."

The unusual emphasis upon family life in the Mormon culture is partially accounted for by this doctrine. In addition, as previous chapters have established, the Church is designed as the center for family social and recreational activities throughout

227

the week, making Mormonism a total experience instead of a Sunday morning exercise. Therefore, pressure brought to bear upon the unmarried has its base in the social structure of Mormonism as well as in the doctrine.

Of course, the concept of a society without the structure of marriage and the family unit is incomprehensible to most people even if they recognize the need for some acceptable alternative arrangements. Society, in its search for order, made the natural human tendency toward family grouping the principle upon which Western civilization is based. "Order" included "protecting" women by controlling their sexuality, which led to the establishment of the traditional Catholic position of allowing equal respect for motherhood and virginity. Marriage in the Catholic Church is encouraged for the purpose of responsible parenthood, but the single state, assuming sexual abstinence, is honored as well. And while birth control is opposed by the Catholic Church, its members are free from pressure to marry and produce children, and their spiritual development toward a state of grace is strictly an individual matter. With various modifications, the Protestant churches adhere also to this traditional philosophy of marriage.

Marriage in the Jewish view, on the other hand, is as important as it is to the Mormons, though its importance is of a different nature. Here the marriage relationship itself is valued, the totality in sharing and wholeness found therein being important steps toward finding God. With the home as sanctuary, emphasis is upon earthly fulfillment, for to the Jewish people eternity represents but a hope. While children are cherished, procreation is not the primary purpose of the Jewish marriage union. According to Rabbi Abner Bergman of Salt Lake City, the commandment to "replenish the earth" is interpreted loosely in modern-day Judaism to mean "produce your own kind." He explains that, without a hierarchical structure, such questions as birth control and abortion are matters of individual judgment.

It is interesting to note that the pressure toward marriage in the Jewish faith is placed almost entirely upon the male, with the unmarried state of the female considered simply an unfortunate circumstance. Rabbi Bergman acknowledges that in the tradition of attaching greater significance to the male development in the culture, Judaism is not without its discriminating aspects. But nevertheless, it leaves the Jewish woman with her options.

The fact is that marital status is not an operative concern of most major religious organizations of the world. Among doctrinal variations of the patriarchal biblical theme, none but the Mormon denies the choice to remain single. Yet a society that does not permit women to freely initiate courtship and marriage does not grant all women the choice to be married, leaving the single Mormon woman in a particularly difficult position.

If emphasis upon marriage has created a stressful situation for single members of contemporary Mormon society, the nineteenth-century plural marriage system did at least offer the solution to that problem. The single sisters only became a casualty of the Latter-day Saint marriage plan after "the professedly free and liberal American government violated their official oaths by prohibiting polygamy," taking away what Mormons considered their "inherent rights and privileges guaranteed by the Constitution."[1] Otherwise, the Saints could have continued providing each woman the opportunity to marry and produce children, fulfilling the religious commitments which would secure her place in the Celestial Kingdom.

Duty-bound and eager to build their individual kingdoms in the eternal world, many Latter-day Saint males in this mutually advantageous plural marriage arrangement gladly accepted additional wives from among available females. The righteousness of the system was emphasized regularly by Brigham Young, who explained its greater purpose in the following sermon:

If my wife had borne me all the children that she would ever bear, the Celestial Law would teach me to take young women that would have children. Do you understand this? I have told you many times that there are multitudes of pure and holy spirits waiting to take tabernacles (bodies). Now what is our duty?[2]

230

It was further reinforced in that sermon by the Prophet that those waiting spirits should be borne into Mormon homes to prevent them from entering into "families of the wicked, where they would be trained in wickedness, debauchery, and every species of crime."

Taking into consideration what the women had at stake in the Celestial marriage plan, it is of little wonder that the nineteenth-century "Mormon feminists" rose up to defend it and called the prohibition of polygamy a travesty of women's rights. Their feminist uprising easily can be recognized as cooperation in a political maneuver by the patriarchy for their personal advantage, with the women's deliberate attempt to overcome their poor image as a part of that scheme. But their women's rights platform also had deep personal and emotional meaning to the sisters involved. In fact, in the long run, the Latter-day Saint women who were left without husbands were truly persecuted in a religious sense by the enactment of the anti-polygamy law.

If we return to the nineteenth century to take another look at the Mormon women's advocacy of women's rights at that time, we see that, because of their uniquely Mormon notion of marriage as religious commitment and as a means to eternal salvation in the kingdom of God, they naturally had related emancipation of women everywhere to a system that offered each the opportunity for respectable marriage. From their specialized view of the world, these Mormon theoretical feminists had been presenting in their plural marriage plan what they considered the most practical and satisfying answer for women of the world. It was no doubt in the true spirit of sisterhood that the Mormon sisters expressed particular compassion for the single women in the monogamous system which they described as a "tyrannical system of vices and social evils." Helen Mar Whitney had the best interests of the single women in mind when she wrote in *Why We Practice Plural Marriage* about the "hypocritical" monogamous situation.

A man steals away from his house in the dark to indulge in dishonorable and degrading passions in secret places, and then abandons the partner of his guilty pleasure to a life of wretchedness, shame, and want while he seeks another victim.[3]

The sympathetic Mrs. Whitney explained that such women were left with no alternative but licentiousness "which they knew to be sin," a pitfall that would not have occurred in polygamy, where "every woman is designed to be the glory of some man instead of the object of his wanton pleasure."

Mormon feminists were puritanical feminists. As we have noted it was the combination of their conception of women's rights with moral integrity that made them boast the superiority of their plural marriage system, "if people would be honest enough to admit it." Not only could they claim that plural marriage eliminated the need for male infidelity, but for them it also eliminated the need for women to be reduced to the status of courtesan or prostitute, and none would be forced to spend a lifetime of penury. Admitting that they were not entirely free from "trials and vexations," the Mormon sisters said that with all women married they "at least had the satisfaction of knowing that their husbands would not violate their sacred marriage vows."

Championing the single woman, Mormon sisters promoted widespread conversion to polygamy for her protection, submitting a theory to account for the needed reform. Adam, according to their theory, had only one woman because he and Eve were created perfect in health and morals, but as ancient laws and ordinances were changed by man, people became imperfect. Had everyone "fulfilled the measure of his creation" as commanded, there would have been husbands for all womankind. However, as man began to multiply upon earth, the number of women exceeded the number of men (a statistical assertion of questionable validity at the time it was made). Therefore, a social system adapted to this imperfect condition was regarded as a practical necessity. Furthermore, the sisters reasoned, "If love (physical) be refining and ennobling and the birthright of all, yet the Creator has restricted its indulgence to the marriage relation, then certainly marriage must be the right of all." They called it "absurd" for anyone to think that a benevolent God would have made no provisions for everyone to be married. The fault, apparent to Mormon polygamists, was not in nature or God's laws, but in the social system.[4]

To the dismay of feminists, there always have been men who refer to woman's "proper sphere." But to those who chose to "harp upon that theme," the Mormon "feminists" answered that it was the men themselves who were responsible for preventing women from filling that sphere. They charged that because of the denial by men of God's plural marriage law, thousands of women were forced to seek employment outside the home, the sphere "they would have been only too glad to occupy." In a dramatic plea for feminine justice that missed the point of true feminist interests, the Mormon sisters continued:

With marriage impossible for half of its women, society not only discriminates against them, it declares war on them. Now let this warfare cease and let woman have her rights—a husband and a home! We must prevent the suffering of the single woman![5]

Helen Whitney, one of the women encouraged by the church leadership to defend polygamy on behalf of Mormon women, set forth proposals which were supported and likely inspired by Mormon men as well. Brigham Young, self-proclaimed women's rights advocate, had this to add to their defense:

If the Prophet had said, "Brother Brigham, you can never have but one wife at a time," I should have said, "Glory Hallelujah, that is just what I like!" But, he said, "You will have to take more than one wife, and this order has to spread and increase until the inhabitants of the earth repent of their evils and men will do what is right toward the females." Also I say, "Hallelujah!"[6]

How many single women in nineteenth-century America secretly would have been willing to accept a husband-sharing arrangement? Were polygamy advocates correct in assuming that "even a small share of care and attention of a good husband would be far better than no husband at all"? There was hardly a groundswell toward the movement, but it is possible that such a compromise might have represented an improvement in some lives. With limited professional and employment opportunities, certainly life for many unmarried women of the American working class left much to be desired. Mrs. Whitney made a reasonably valid point when she suggested to the "charitable sisters of the East who found polygamy such an abomination," that if they had "sympathy to spare, they should use it on women who were factory workers there." She rightly pointed out that in Mormon Zion there were not only marriage possibilities, but with the task of building the kingdom there were greater opportunities for gainful employment of women as well.[7]

While the valiant efforts of Mormon feminists on

behalf of single women were laudable, feminist philosophy, of course, has never recognized the basic Mormon premise that marriage is the ultimate goal for all women. It is unlikely, however, that the majority of Americans understood the significance of the Mormon marriage laws in which Mormon-style feminism was rooted. Nor did the polygamists understand why the Federal government chose to persecute them while taking no steps to "punish the wicked army of defenders in monogamy." Such treatment, they felt, was "unjust, unphilosophical, and unworthy a liberal, enlightened age."[8]

Obviously, conversion to the "loathsome monogamous system" eliminated the Mormon "utopia" for single women. Like women they had pitied in monogamy, Mormon sisters were left to compete for available men in the Church. But, in addition to enduring the hardships to which singles are subjected throughout society, they had the burden of coping with the problem of eternal salvation. For what remained after the demise of polygamy was a family-oriented church with the eternal marriage law intact.

Circulated occasionally were stories of older single women being married and "sealed" to male members of the Church to allay their anxiety of facing death without the comfort of belonging to an eternal family of the Celestial Kingdom. But for much of the twentieth century the Mormon Church treated the unresolved singles problem with benign neglect,

236

offering little more than sympathetic counseling from the married bishops of the wards.

However, in the 1970s, responding to current needs of a rapidly growing church, some structural changes were initiated which included special programs for single members. In changes directed toward maintaining Mormon cohesiveness, singles were organized under the name of "special interests" as part of the MPMIA.* Acknowledging that "a swelling single sisterhood within the Church presented a growing problem," Elder Marion Hanks introduced the new plan by explaining:

Every lovely woman has a dream and a purpose in her life of fulfillment in a home and family. As a church, we appropriately emphasize this and try to help accentuate the importance of preparing for that goal. But the fact is that a great many do not enjoy these privileges.[9]

Reassured that there was "yet much they could become and contribute," singles were presented with a program designed to help them develop as individuals. "What we are saying," said Elder Hanks, "is that a great many wonderful people are going to have attention paid to them."[10]

To carry out the recreational and educational programs designed for singles only, special "singles wards" were established. Even the traditional Mon-

*Melchizdek Priesthood Mutual Improvement Association

day "family home evening" was arranged under the direction of a bishop for single members who could not meet with legitimate families. The goal was to involve everyone, Mormon-style, in activities and service programs to provide a sense of belonging.

Not long after the program for singles was launched, however, leaders deemed it appropriate to warn of the danger in the "colonization of members." Noting that many interpret "special interests" to mean "special problems," Elder Hanks, in the 1975 MPMIA conference, urged the membership to "respond to them as individuals with problems, not problem individuals."[11] Then Elder James C. Faust defined some of the special problems faced by Mormon adults who had never married.

They often feel as being suspect. That is, being suspected of something being wrong with them. They feel looked upon as being unorthodox, being unrighteous, being immature and irresponsible, as well as not progressing spiritually.[12]

Elder Faust concluded his remarks with the statement that "it is unfair to apply these assumptions to *all* adult singles." Skits were presented at the 1975 MPMIA Conference portraying problems of Mormon singles with suggested solutions, characteristic Mormon solutions of more church involvement. And in a message to "special interests" people whose "needs admittedly have been neglected because the Church properly has been oriented toward family and marriage," Elder Faust told them nevertheless they are loved by the Lord and the President of the Church. Then he added, apparently without awareness of connotations of a well-known ethnic cliché, "Some of our choicest members belong to this group."[13]

After its first year the singles program was declared a success by the Church leaders, who pronounced themselves proud that never had there been more concern for or greater opportunities offered to adult singles than now. Possible insight into why sudden recognition had occurred was given by Mormon singles program director Jeffrey Holland when he explained to the membership that "single adults across the nation today seem to be seeking a counter-culture as they withdraw from society." This, he told them, was not so in the LDS Church because they had been offered the MPMIA program.

Newsworthy, too, was the successful integration of singles into the Relief Society, previously identified primarily with activities for married women. In fact, the *Salt Lake Tribune* featured an article and picture of Relief Society President Barbara Smith in June 1975 with the caption "Single People Contribute." And in tribute to the general accomplishments of the Church in recognizing its single members, Elder Faust related this story in the June 1975 MPMIA Conference:

The other day we heard of a young lady who seemed to be having a marvelous time. She said, "I have decided I can be someone, even if I am not able to be someone's."

Statements and rhetoric concerning the innovative new program for Mormon singles, indeed the mere fact of the need for such a program, served to dramatize the extent to which the Mormon Church functions as a social-family institution and the degree to which singles are isolated within it, a situation unparalleled in any other religious organization. Nevertheless, director Holland insisted, "We are and always must be a family church," and he explained that "part of the genius of this new program is that it includes single members within the greater church family, even though they do not have husbands, wives or children."[14]

There is indeed genius in a program which succeeds in helping people avoid loneliness, but apparently there is not sufficient genius to provide a way to the Celestial Kingdom for Mormons who never marry. So while many older singles, the divorced and widowed, found some social satisfaction in the newly organized activities on their behalf, and young single adults whose social life centered in the Church applauded a change that turned Church events into social mixers, others were not so enthusiastic. Admitting that the Church leadership deserved some credit for "recognizing that singles exist and trying to do something constructive about them," many thought their program of "super caring" succeeded only in making the problem more acute. "Singles' wards are a nightmare," said one woman who added that while there she felt as if she were "on the auction block."[15] Director Holland had reminded members that the MPMIA activities were not designed to be used as a marriage bureau, but there was a general feeling among singles interviewed that the Mormon preoccupation with marriage made the "mating arena" atmosphere difficult to avoid. The "special interests" program could hardly be labeled successful on a large scale because the attendance has been described as heavily weighted with women "complete with hope chests and the Mormon marriage complex."

In spite of Church teachings, there are Mormons who choose the single life, one of whom confided to me that she prefers having ward members feel sorry for her to letting them know she made that unacceptable decision. Satisfied with having chosen to be a business executive, she acknowledged that there is no place for her choice within the confines of a church that only values the career of married homemaker. And because of what she considers her divergent views and interests, she found very few like herself at the singles' ward. She lamented:

My idea of church is a place where there are little kids, grandmas, singles and married people all worshipping together. Each individual should be able to communicate with God and achieve within her own limits to become the best person she can be.[16]

The notion that spiritual fulfillment must come through a husband's priesthood is an offensive con-

241

cept to many and for some dissident women is a
source of serious conflict with Church doctrine. "The
idea that some guy is needed to save your soul is
preposterous"[17] was one interpretation of the Church
policy. Critical too of the counseling system, some
say that lay bishops, all of whom must be married,
are ill-equipped to deal with problems of singles in
the Church. With their commitment to the Church
position and minimal training in counseling techniques, they often merely add to the pressure.

While reasons are many and varied for members to
drift from religion, interviews with several inactive
Mormon singles suggested that in one way or
another it was their "singleness" that had driven
them away from the LDS Church. For some there was
just the vague discomfort of not fitting in, known in
the Church as the "back-row syndrome," while
others claim there is very little of interest for them,
even with the new program. One inactive Mormon
single, who defined the Church attitude toward
singles as the sole reason for her leaving, explained:

As it is today, the Church disenfranchises me as a human
being. It has alienated me and people like me.[18]

To these alienated women the "special interests"
program represents a superficial attempt at pacifica-
tion when in fact "it would take nothing short of a
doctrinal change for the Church to regard singles as
people."[19] None of the women I interviewed expects

that change to be forthcoming, but several women suggested that one reasonable alternative would be for the Church leaders to "slow down the pressure."

But deemphasizing marriage is obviously not the intention of the present-day leadership. Ironically, the women's movement, which likely influenced some Mormon singles to begin verbalizing their feelings, at the same time caused a reactionary increase in pressure from the Church. Leaving no question about the importance of the marriage issue, President Spencer Kimball, in October 1974, frankly called it "selfishness, cold and self-centered, which leads people to shun marriage responsiblity." And the marriage policy of the Church has been confirmed by authorities in every LDS Conference held in the 1970s with such messages as:

We say again to all people: We members of the Church marry! All normal couples should become parents! The Lord did not give man sex as a plaything. We were placed on earth not primarily to have fun and to satisfy our passion in a life of selfishness.[20]

Reflecting Mormon obedience, the Utah birthrate continues to be remarkably high, often the highest in the country. But again, in another example of what some consider inappropriately timed statements, the Mormon Church reacted to the current issue of world over-population by stressing the importance for Mormons to continue producing large families. To young Mormons in San Diego, California, in the spring of 1975, President Kimball explained:

...the spirits are waiting there with our Heavenly Father to come here to finish this part of the plan. Have you ever had to stand in line? You get tired of it. That's what many of the choice spirits are doing now—waiting to come here.[21]

He advised the elders (young men) there to find the right girl, enter the temple and be married. "Let no single man excuse himself by rationalizing with his own concepts."

Church education programs continue to condition young women for their "high callings as wives and mothers," and rarely does a current LDS conference neglect to emphasize eternal salvation through marriage. At a recent gathering President Kimball praised women who accept their femininity and responsibility for bearing and rearing children, and reminded them:

The role of woman was fixed when she was created. You have learned from infancy what is right.... Marriage is *essential* in order to obtain the Celestial Kingdom of God.[22]

Turning then to the singles of the audience he offered then a word of comfort. "Those who through no fault of their own fail to marry will not be *condemned* by the Lord for anything he or she could not have helped." But along with that consolation came some advice for single women. Noting that a number of the women "appear well-groomed, worthy and most desirable" he addressed them with these thoughts:

If it is not working—if you have had fewer opportunities than you expected, you need to take a careful inventory of yourself. Evaluate your habits, your speech, your appearance, your weight, and your eccentricities if you have them. Do all you can to right your wrongs and achieve your proper goals.[23]

Echoing the sentiments of the Mormon patriarchy in a book entitled *The Singular Life*, Carol Clark, a devoted Mormon woman, writes of ways in which she and other single women have adapted to their compromised position of "working with the principle instead of the practice of marriage." Clark maintains that "doing what one can to attain a righteous companion through temple marriage is the ranking obligation of all single sisters." Admitting unashamedly that nothing is more difficult for her to come to grips with than the fact that she may not marry, she deals with her adversity by setting goals that act as a complement to marriage:

I have learned to bake bread, do needlepoint, and quilt. I have a sense of fulfillment and know I'll be a better wife and mother because of the things I'm doing.[24]

Believing that it is "the business of all LDS women to uphold the priesthood in every way," this single author poses the question: "How then shall a sister without the leadership of a priesthood-holding husband be steadfast enough to see the salvation of the Lord in her own life?" Turning then to another principle of Mormon philosophy, that of self-improvement, her book proceeds as a "how-to" guide. In outlining a program for emotional, spiritual and physical development that will "serve the woman well in case the end is not accomplished," she parrots President Kimball's suggestions and includes additional practical tips concerning social skills and money management. Among important don'ts, she mentions the pitfall of marrying out of the Church, which is to be avoided by resisting the temptation of dating non-Mormons. Also, "Don't succumb to bitterness and depression," she warns, "and don't listen to feminist groups. There is nothing in the gospel of Jesus Christ that limits the single woman," she writes.[25]

On the other hand, Carol Clark is a woman who finds chasing any miscellaneous man demeaning. "I don't ever want to reach the point of anxiety that I would condescend to marry just anyone," she emphasizes. But there is evidence to suggest that some Mormons have been doing just that. Despite relatively strong divorce laws, the Utah divorce rate consistently hovers near the top of the national scale. Perhaps, with little in common besides their religious orientation toward marriage, such couples meet and marry at an early age. Utah statistics show the rate of teen-age marriage and divorce well above the national average.

Apparently failing to consider the possible "spin-off" effect of their marriage policy, Church officials alternately advise members not to delay marriage and condemn the high divorce rate. Again, selfishness was given as the cause of divorce by President Kimball who termed "specious" the argument that children are better off in single homes than in fighting homes. "There need be no battling parents," he admonished in the 1974 Conference. As the above statistics confirm, however, the unfavorable disposition of the Church toward divorce has been ineffective in preventing it. That divorce must be occasionally tolerated is explained in Bruce R. McConkie's book, *Mormon Doctrine:*

In the gospel view, all marriages should be eternal, and divorce should never enter the picture. But since all men, as a result of apostasy and inequity, are not living the full and perfect gospel, the Lord permits divorce and allows dissolution of the marriage union.[26]

On divorce, in the LDS conference of 1975 Elder James Faust contributed his opinion, which is widely accepted by LDS authorities, that its seeds are often sown and the blessings of the children delayed by wives working outside the home. Calling it a "tragedy of greatest proportion," he urged that divorce be avoided at "almost any cost."

If at any cost it cannot be avoided, divorce is granted at a high cost to Mormon women. Unless the estranged couple of a temple marriage is willing to resume partnership in the eternal world, they must seek to break the seal that binds them through temple divorce. In so doing the woman forfeits her place in the Celestial Kingdom, and the children of the union remain sealed to their father as part of his individual kingdom in heaven. The male may readily take another eternal partner, but it is usually conceded that a second marriage for a woman is for time only and not for eternity. However, special permission occasionally may be granted by Church officials for a woman's second eternal marriage, depending on the worthiness of the individual and the circumstances. Because cases are judged on an individual basis, specific conditions of temple divorce and remarriage are not described in books of doctrine. But Mormon divorce like Mormon marriage is more complex than for most non-Mormons because it involves the status of an individual in the life hereafter, and again the Mormon woman is affected more deeply in a negative sense. Her feelings of guilt and ostracism must be exceeded only by the loss of her children in the eternal world and her place in the Celestial Kingdom.

With awareness of some problems arising from

these complexities, the provocative title of "Un-married in a Married Church," which has been adopted here, was selected for a panel discussion at the 1975 Women's Conference at Brigham Young University in Provo, Utah. Of the four participants, two were single and two were widows. One of the latter hastened to defend her position as that of being eternally married in the church view. She considered herself technically not representative of the problems the title suggested. Both widows focused only upon difficulties encountered in adjusting to the Mormon social institution without a partner, concluding generally that the problems were within themselves, and not within the Church.

Of the singles, one was a teacher at the university who outlined ways in which singles might strive to destroy Church myths about them, naming non-participants, transients, and persons who do not relate to families as common stereotypes. But the issue of her eternal salvation was not raised during her presentation. Having struggled with the possibility that her position in the Church might be in jeopardy, the second single panelist had sought counsel from her bishop. Satisfied and enlightened by the counsel she received, she shared it with the group. Without a husband, she would take priesthood guidance from the bishopric of her ward, and being without a family of her own, the ward families would serve as substitute. That this greater church family arrangement would not include her in the Celestial Kingdom was unmentioned, by nature, no doubt, of being unresolved.

Having as its primary purpose the teaching of the Mormon gospel, Brigham Young University has not been highly regarded for its academic freedom. None of the participants challenged or criticized the Church's policy toward singles or women in general. Instead they dodged and rationalized the delicate, controversial issue. In fact, at this very unusual women's conference by today's university standards, the women closed each meeting by confirming their loyalty to the all-male priesthood.

But the best the Church can offer to single Mormon women in return for that loyalty is the following nonspecific promise for their otherwise specifically defined Mormon eternal world. The message comes to "the good sisters who are single and alone" from *Doctrines of Salvation* by former Church President Joseph Fielding Smith:

... You are not under any obligation of accepting some proposal that comes to you which is distasteful for fear of condemnation. If in your hearts you feel that the gospel is true, and would under proper conditions receive these ordinances and sealing blessings in the temple of the Lord (marry); and that is your faith and your hope and your desire, and that does not come to you now; the Lord will make it up, and you shall be blessed—for no blessing shall be withheld.[27]

In effect, if a woman is not guilty of "thought crime" as Orwell describes it in *1984*, that is, if she truly wants to be married, this will be taken into consideration by the Lord. For her no blessings shall be withheld except, of course, the ultimate blessing of entrance into the highest kingdom of God, the Celestial Kingdom, because the Church emphasizes that this would be impossible. That leaves then a bleak situation indeed for the Mormon woman who dares to choose to be single.

Woman was made to be a help to a man. But she was not fitted to be a help to man except in generation, because another man would prove a more effective help in anything else.

Thomas Aquinas

10

REVELATION OR REVOLUTION

The Mormon culture can be viewed as a patriarchal microcosm in which the history of women is one of subtle subversion. Although the unique features of its doctrine set the Latter-day Saint Church apart from other religious organizations regarding the status of women, the difference in patriarchal control is only a matter of degree. To the outside observer, there may be a particular madness in Mormon businessmen interpreting God's wishes for women on a daily basis, but it really is no more ludicrous in the long view than patriarchal leaders of any faith presumptuously outlining, through the ages, women's duties according to God. Traditions of other patriarchies may seem more logical only because of their antiquity.

Women obviously have the special capacity to be mothers. From that biological fact, male ecclesiastic leaders have constructed over the centuries elaborate religious systems of rules and regulations to which women have been expected to adhere. As far as anthropologists and archaeologists have been able to determine, societies throughout the world prior to about 5,000 years B.C. held the reproductive power of women in such awe that it commanded religious worship. Thus, these ancient cultures worshipped a Mother Goddess. We can only speculate about the circumstances that led from Mother Goddess worship to the worship of God the Father and endowed males with ecclesiastic power. In ancient mythology there is the strong suggestion that males deeply coveted woman's birth-giving capacity. It might be said that there was evidence of widespread "womb-envy." Puberty rites of ancient cultures quite regularly re-enacted the birth process, portraying the male as the begetter of the child, and their myths featured some truly remarkable births indeed. Athena, for instance, was born in full armor from Zeus's head and Dionysus gestated in Zeus's thigh! And of course, as the myth goes, Eve emerged from Adam's rib.

Sheila Collins in *A Different Heaven and Earth*

presents an interesting discussion of the myths and theories that relate to the development of patriarchies. According to her examples, from both ancient mythology and the Bible, there were signs of political-religious power struggles between males and females. Many anthropologists support the theory that ultimately male supremacy was achieved simply as a result of man's superior physical strength. They believe that males and females were naturally drawn to certain activities because of their physical characteristics. But some also subscribe to the theory that the transition to God the Father worship coincided with the male's discovery of his role in the procreative process. This discovery, it has been conjectured, reduced woman's role from its highly elevated status to that of a mere "receptacle" for male seed and gave males the double advantage of physical superiority and reproductive power. The woman's role in reproduction was not fully appreciated for thousands of years after that. Perhaps as Hebrew males planted their seed in various receptacles it became obvious that in order for them to claim their own offspring they would need to take possession of and exercise control over their receptacles. Thus, in response to this societal need for order, God the Father was put in charge of the world and man was put in charge of woman.

As clergymen today perpetuate such notions as man is the head and the woman has the duty to be his helpmate, and as they further dwell upon the particulars of woman's homemaking responsibilities, the majority might be criticized more for their philosophical limitations than for their motives in regard to power. Nevertheless, failure to fulfill these "God-given" obligations can be relied upon to produce guilt in women, and with guilt being the essence of religious experience, patriarchies have managed to create and maintain social control based on that principle.

In the case of the Mormon patriarchs, with their assumption that allowing women to make other than designated choices will cause the demise of the family, there is an almost pathetic attempt to preserve an institution that does not really work very well in its present restrictive form, as divorce statistics within their own kingdom point up. Not only is it naive to expect that marital love and commitment can be dictated by religious laws, but paradoxically, by insisting that men and women adhere to the traditional stereotyped roles in marriage today, the patriarchy contributes significantly to its failure.

This is not to suggest that the granting of equal status and freedom for women necessarily would lower the divorce rate, but undoubtedly such social conditions would improve the marriages that survive. And marriages in which the woman has a subordinate role, unless that is by her own choice, very likely are not worthy of preservation. A reasonable assumption can be made that the degree to which a woman is allowed to experience full freedom and

255

equality determines her capability in achieving a satisfying and mature relationship. In fact, a marriage relationship based upon any principle other than full equality is inconceivable to those who have achieved that goal.

Actually, many Mormon marriages have been successful in balancing the power between husband and wife, and in reality, that balance is often tipped in the woman's favor. Because the strong Mormon women have assumed the responsibility of keeping husbands and children involved in the Church, the culture, in fact, shows matriarchal tendencies. Nevertheless, the philosophy of the patriarchy in regard to male authority pervades the atmosphere of a Latter-day Saint community, and even if operatively that authority in the home is largely ceremonial, a system that sanctions the priesthood-holding husband as an authority figure is a potentially destructive system for both men and women.

Additionally, in the patriarchal restriction of women's roles for the sake of preserving the family, for which today's Mormon patriarchs are especially noted, there is hidden an outrageous assertion that without legal and religious restraints women would stop nurturing their children properly. Contrary to the assumptions of the male leaders, there is evidence that the successful nurturing of children can be accomplished in a variety of ways other than by the mother becoming a full-time homemaker. From a broad survey recently conducted by Jean Curtis for her book *Working Mothers* (1975), she concluded that children of working mothers often develop greater independence and self-reliance and are more likely to seek higher education. Psychological theory today generally does not recognize the necessity of mother remaining in the home, except in the child's early years. Many psychologists agree that a more important factor relating to successful child-rearing is whether the mother is happy in her work.

Among the many indignities women have suffered over the years in male-dominated societies, it is the lack of confidence in her judgment regarding her own affairs implied by controlling religious laws that provides cause for genuine anger. By protecting women from themselves, the patriarchies relay the message that essentially women are not to be trusted with freedom or power, which is both an undermining of woman's integrity and a basic assault on her humanness. Power, of course, is corruptive, and women are corruptible, and freedom no doubt would be exploited by some, but in truth, women very likely have the same capacity for good and evil as men and in any case should be granted the opportunity to exercise and demonstrate that capacity.

It goes without saying that society's male power systems could not have flourished through the centuries without the consent of the subordinates. Today, however, some of that consent is being withheld. With an inevitability as great as for the survival of civilization, American women will enter

257

the twenty-first century having acquired equal rights under the law and at least a respectable, if not equal, share of leadership power. Out of the history of subordination some remnants of prejudice against women will of course remain; but, because of the full-scale women's movement now in progress, the status of women will be considerably improved.

Forgetting the resistance, the hostility, and the insults inflicted upon the vocal feminists of our day, a majority of the citizens of America can be expected eventually to take pride collectively in their country's progress toward establishing equitable policies for women. Certainly most Americans by now have conceded that the passing of the woman's suffrage law in 1920 was a noble act, even though the women in the forefront of that struggle were hardly viewed with affection.

Similarly, although it was the result of a destructive war, Americans generally acknowledge that righteousness prevailed in the land when Black slavery was abolished, and only occasionally contemplate how such an abomination could have been permitted in a democratic experiment in the first place. And after the country stops trembling from the violence of the civil rights movement of the 1960s, Americans no doubt will feel national pride in the opportunities that were provided for oppressed minorities as a result of that revolution. Such is the gradual pattern of social reform.

In the slow process of altering the national consensus toward accomplishing social justice, history has demonstrated that legislation has been an important first step. But it also has left no doubt that discriminatory attitudes that have been harbored in a society are not easily eliminated by law. With societal attitudes regarding women's roles so deeply rooted in the Judeo-Christian tradition, the mere passage of a suffrage law, while a magnanimous gesture to be sure, obviously was insufficient to yield to many American women the equality they had anticipated. Hence, their continued dissatisfaction gave rise to the current women's movement, the second such movement within the century, and the importance and irreversibility of the feminist movement today has been validated by the increasing hysterical resistance to it.

Continuing in the pursuit of more options for women, the primary task of today's feminists remains to surmount the sexual stereotypes of religious tradition. Many of those comfortably situated in traditional male-female roles have asked why women, satisfied with their position as wife and mother for thousands of years, must now, in this century, demand a change. Such critics fail to take into account that the accelerated rate of change of our times, so graphically described in Alvin Toffler's *Future Shock*, separates contemporary man (and woman) from all others before them. From Toffler's discussions of the impermanence and the technological advances of the twentieth century, all of which can be readily observed, it is easy to see how the rapidly changing society has radically altered the needs of women in particular.

Apparently oblivious to the hard realities, many patriarchal leaders, well-armed with scripture, continue to exercise their power in this regard, convincing multitudes that it is still a woman's responsibility to confine herself to the roles defined in the Bible. Therefore, while the church properly serves as a stabilizing force in a chaotic world, such interpretations of scripture by the clergy of any faith or denomination serve to intensify the problems of women.

Many established traditions no doubt made sense in the beginning, but much in the Bible regarding women's roles, as in other aspects of modern life, simply is not relevant today. Population growth was promoted in the Bible for a world where survival amongst warring tribes often depended upon sheer numbers, but unlimited population growth today, in a world short of resources, has been recognized as inappropriate and irresponsible. In any case, debating how scripture should influence the lives of women today might be considered a moot question. Feminist philosophers and theologians strongly reject the notion that the Bible, which has been so blatantly shorn of female imagery, should be considered the word of God. A new wave of feminist "theologizers" today is proceeding with the basic premise that whoever or whatever God is, the message that emanates from the Great Spirit could not be a sexist message.

Even if patriarchal leaders are strictly guided by the Bible and are prevented from altering scriptural meaning by their fundamentalist religious laws, they still have the power to alter the lives of people by their choices and emphases. For instance, it is well-known that women are less restricted by the New Testament when emphasis by the clergy is shifted from the teachings attributed to Paul to the teachings of Jesus. Leonard Swidler's article entitled "Jesus Was a Feminist" (1971) points out with many examples how Jesus disregarded the established conventions and taboos in his relationships with women. Instead of showing the traditional Hebrew insubordination of women, he treated them with equality and respect.[1] Unfortunately that clear message to women from Jesus was lost or distorted as it was relayed by Christian patriarchs. Thus, it has become obvious, because of the possibilities therein, that fair interpretations of scripture can be assured only when churches are guided by human beings of both sexes.

Though incomprehensible to many people at the present time, it is the essence and the most serious aspiration of feminism today that the current women's movement will mark the beginning of the end of patriarchal societies. That full realization of this objective is a long way off, in fact that it likely will

261

not occur in their lifetime, is understood. It is encouraging, however, that within only a decade the slow process of integration has begun. Only the Catholic Church, the Mormon Church, and a few orthodox and fundamentalist groups officially continue to resist totally the principle of women's leadership and equality in the church.

Though it remained firm in its position, the Roman Catholic Church acknowledged in September 1977 the increasing importance of the woman question. This was the occasion of Pope Paul's eightieth birthday. Reporting from the Vatican, the Associated Press singled out papal resistance to the ordination of women among the reasons "ecumenical dialogue had soured" at that time. In the face of the progress made to date, it is unlikely that the patriarchal world view will endure indefinitely, However, the coming to power of an enlightened and creative Catholic leader, comparable to the late Pope John, could provide the necessary break-through for women in this important societal transition.

But, as has been noted throughout this book, the vital ecumenical dialogue that has soured among members of the Catholic hierarchy has not even begun in the Mormon Church. And while their current preoccupation with stressing women's "proper roles" suggests a certain anxiety about the subject, Mormon authorities clearly have indicated their intentions to keep their system intact. Needless to say, the arbitrary position taken by Mormon leaders regarding women's roles is by no means as pivotal in reversing the patriarchal trend in Western society as that of the Catholics. Nevertheless, the aggressive use of Mormon wealth and power to impede progress is potentially threatening to women everywhere and has provided reason for overwhelming national concern.

The extent to which the male-dominated Latter-day Saint system is accepted or tolerated by Mormon women themselves is ultimately their own decision. Regardless of pressure from outside, change must come from within. With their church so elaborately designed on a base of male domination, both on earth and in heaven, Mormonism stands out among religions of the world as one least able to establish true equality of the sexes. For reasons which we have discussed, Mormon women, in spite of their remarkable history and their claims to superior opportunities, cannot be accommodated readily into the priesthood and leadership of the Church.

The manner in which the Mormons handle their unusual situation in regard to the woman question will be interesting to observe. Even as they have expanded into a large worldwide empire, the Saints have preserved much of the cohesiveness that has served them well in the past in their various unpopular stands against the outside world. And with its inherent provisions for filling many basic human needs, Mormonism has demonstrated an amazing capacity to endure.

Under the protection and strict control of the Church, the Saints in this American-spawned religion are provided with the illusion of freedom and in their Church-sanctioned pursuit of personal power and material success, they are allowed the creative expression of their innate aggression. This is a condition that Sigmund Freud viewed as imperative and therefore as justification for capitalism.[2] But among the humanly satisfying innovations most responsible for the success of the Mormon culture, ironically, was the granting of ecclesiastic power to virtually all male members which, according to Dennis Michael Quinn in his doctoral thesis entitled *The Mormon Hierarchy*, "appealed to the bourgeois envy of aristocracy power."[3] Since power must be exercised over someone, the granting of equal power to women would cancel out and thus destroy that unique advantage. But who could have anticipated in 1830 that one day women would develop a bourgeois envy of aristocracy power themselves?

If the twentieth-century thrust toward woman power could not have been anticipated in the formative years of the Mormon Church, it is barely comprehensible to the Mormon leadership even now. Of the many factors relating to the status of Mormon women, it bears emphasis that with the average age of the Council of Twelve well into the seventies, the members of the governing body of the Church are products of an earlier age. They have accumulated maturity and wisdom from lifetime experiences, but their experiences have been vastly different from those of a large percentage of the membership today, and sermons at Latter-day Saint conferences often convey not merely a generation gap but a chasm between the elderly authorities and the population at large.

It must be remembered that in the innovative days of Mormonism, the Saints were guided by a Prophet in his twenties who was a martyred Prophet by the age of thirty-five. And when Brigham Young assumed the leadership at forty-three, he was a man in the prime of life. But Brother Brigham was so durable that he reigned over the Mormon kingdom for thirty-two years, and if members of his council awaited an opportunity to serve in his post, they grew old in the process.

In 1877, after the death of Brigham Young, John Taylor became the third President at the age of seventy-two, and Taylor was followed six years later by Wilford Woodruff who was eighty-two. Except for the sixth and seventh Presidents, Joseph F. Smith and Heber J. Grant, who came into power in their sixties, all remaining Prophets have been "set apart" in their seventies or eighties, with one elder recently becoming Prophet at age ninety-two.

Resistance to change is often characteristic of old age, so it is not surprising that the conservative trend in Mormonism, which has replaced the creative spirit of the early Church, has corresponded to the increasing age of the authorities. The power figures in the Vatican belong to the same age category, of course, but Catholic influence, at least in this century, has been confined primarily to matters of religion. With the thorough blending of religion into the political, economic, and social life of the Mormon community, the built-in time gap is of greater significance. Often making the Mormon kingdom seem glaringly out of step with the outside world, this time lag was mentioned frequently by those interviewed for this book as creating a communication problem within the Church.

Therefore, while much attention has been focused in these pages upon the conflicts created for many women by the current restrictive Church leadership, in truth a progressive approach to the woman question could not have been expected by this time from the elderly Mormon authorities. And since obedience to the authorities is a religious priority, the majority of devout followers naturally echo their opinions. Not only has widespread acceptance of the authorities' views been confirmed in interviews with Latter-day Saint women whose lives are centered primarily in the Church, but it has been demonstrated with militance, zeal, and indeed, with a mob spirit which suggests a culture in which individuality is not flourishing.

However, neither the public image projected by conforming Mormons nor the discussions of the restless minority in these chapters to this point have taken into account the large segment of relatively inactive and uninvolved members of the Church who do make individual decisions about their lives. Commonly refered to as "Jack Mormons,"* such members often maintain liaison with the Church as a matter of social convenience or family tradition, and though they may suffer from chronic cases of guilt, they do not adhere strictly to the teachings of the religion. Of this detached group, it is significant to note that if in the past they have merely smiled at the more extreme points of view expressed by Church authorities, many of these casual members recently have become totally alienated by the Church's involvement with right-wing political causes and especially with their stand on women's issues. For some who have taken the middle road in Mormon country, ambivalence has now turned to anger. In fact, the current show of power by the Mormon patriarchy in enforcing its extremely conservative and rigid position regarding women has not only rekindled Gentile antagonism, as we have seen, but it is thought by many to be the most divisive issue within the Mormon Church in this century.

So volatile is the subject that it has provoked some speculation that the continued conservative trend may ultimately lead to a liberal-conservative schism in the Church. Still feeling humiliated by the continued exclusion of Black males from the priesthood,

---

*Originally Jack Mormons were non-Mormons who were sympathetic to the Mormon people. Today Jack Mormon is a popular name given to inactive members of the Church

the liberal faction views the church position on women as further manifestation of grave and probably irreconcilable philosophical differences. Historically, there would be nothing new in the division of a church, with liberal and conservative factions going their separate ways, but even those who have entertained that idea as a Mormon solution concede that the nature of the system makes that possibility remote at least for the present time.

What options are available then for dissenters in the Mormon society, this curious sociological phenomenon in America which has managed to endure as an all-encompassing patriarchal culture? In particular, if women's ideas about their roles in life are in conflict with those of church authorities of the time, what means have they in this system to institute change on their own behalf? Taking into account the remarkable variation in their roles throughout Mormon history and the degree to which their activities have been regulated by the patriarchy from the beginning, this presents an interesting academic question.

The question becomes all the more interesting considering the fact that those most uncomfortable with the current Church policies, while not representing Mormon women in general, most likely do include the majority of women in higher education and professional women whose level of education in many cases surpasses that of the General Authorities of the Church. With their influence being felt in secular affairs of their communities, shouldn't women of this caliber have the capacity to influence the policies of the lay clergy of the Mormon Church? In fact, as the hypothetical question might be posed by feminist philosophers, shouldn't those among them who are most devoted to Mormonism *be* the lay clergy of the Church?

In exploring these questions with Mormon women, two extraordinary patterns emerged. The first was the consistency with which those who are actively involved in the women's movement and define themselves as feminists continue to accept the Mormon patriarchal system with its all-male priesthood, thus evading the issue most vital to feminists of other religious organizations. Although the church policy is recognized as the source of many of their conflicts, discussions about gaining power for women in the Church, except among a few, have been virtually non-existent. Mormon women's rights advocates instead have concentrated their efforts on secular affairs such as the ERA, as we have seen, and yet they ultimately were forced to accept its defeat in Utah as a result of Church influence.

With regard to their roles in the Church, many of these Mormon sisters have ever so gently expressed their hope for the patriarchy's return to a more liberal interpretation of woman's sphere by which they would regain the privileges their nineteenth-century sisters enjoyed. Among the more progressive women of the Church there have been open discussions

269

about a variety of minor improvements in status that they could realistically expect to gain, although some admitted that such recent weak concessions by church leaders as allowing women to sit on the church podium with their dignitary husbands had not been one of their priorities. Very likely, in their failure to acknowledge the essential problem, there is the unspoken futility of women attempting to penetrate a system in which male leadership is so ingrained. But for women to stand on a platform of both feminism and Mormonism is to stand in the middle of the battlefield.

The second unusual aspect of this investigation has been suggested but should be reinforced here. Despite the general undercurrent of dissatisfaction about their situation and the frequent and often emotional expressions of discontent among Mormon women's rights advocates in private conversations or small groups, it has been characteristic for them not only to avoid public airings of their complaints, but, when outsiders are involved, to assume defensive positions. Having been conditioned since the early days of persecution to protect the Mormon image, the Saints have developed a strong ethnic self-consciousness. Even if there were no censorship by the Church, deep in their minds there is a self-censorship which prevents them from saying anything the Church would not wish to have said. In fact, in the heat of the controversy over Mormon policies on women, with public relations an ever-present concern, a Relief Society board member was assigned to formulate and circulate Church policy statements to help members deal appropriately with the non-Mormon press.[4] In this continuing restraint, which stems from a combination of loyalty and fear, the researcher cannot help observing the striking similarity between Mormon sisters of today and those who lived in polygamy in the early days of the Church. In both cases the public defense of the patriarchal teachings often fails to coincide with private confessions to diaries and friends.

Obviously, these conditioned reflexes are the result of an unusually powerful patriarchy and in the best of circumstances would tend to seriously limit the actions of Mormon women who seek equal status in the Church. They also frequently convey the impression to non-Mormons that the women's movement in Mormondom is dead; certainly the International Women's Year meeting in Utah in 1977, distinctive in both size and the number of anti-feminist resolutions, tended to confirm that notion. The curious fact is, however, that the University of Utah's women's conferences, which are philosophically supportive of the women's movement, also have been breaking national attendance records. They were recognized by the country's university women's studies departments in 1975 for that achievement. With both Gentile and Latter-day Saint women turning out en masse for all events, public participation statistics in fact show that there is more activity in Utah, pro and con, in connection with the women's movement than in most other states in the union. The obvious prohibitions against attacking the Mormon power system are observed in the culture, but this record gives an indication of the degree of conflict and public concern the Church has provoked.

Enough anger against current church policies might be generated by Mormon women collectively to plant the seeds of a revolution within the Church, but even if it could survive the system, a revolution of compromised feminism that would permit the patriarchy to retain full power could only bear the most perishable fruit. And to *lead* a feminist movement in this patriarchal society would require the tenacity of an evergreen growing through a rock in the desert. With the existing social pressure and threat of patriarchal reprisal, any woman with a valued position in the community would proceed at great personal risk and corresponding caution. Therefore, ironically, women who care enough about the Church to want to reform it would have too much to lose in the endeavor.

An imaginary situation could be constructed in which it would be possible for Mormon women to make progress toward achieving power in the Church, although the actual occurrence of such an event is inconceivable in Mormondom. From a massive underground operation, an army of Mormon sisters could assemble in one of their famous indignation mass meetings, but this time truly acting on their own behalf. This would be comparable to the way in which armies of Mormon sisters have gathered over the years for the benefit of the Church organization. Demanding priesthood and equality in the Church, this body would be composed of so many prominent and valuable community members that their mass excommunication would be an embarrassment as well as a serious loss to the Church.

The Saints of Mormondom no doubt would be aghast at such an outrageous idea, but before it is dismissed as a preposterous fantasy, they should be reminded that similar Catholic feminist demonstrations have been conducted regularly and have included many revered nuns who openly seek ordination into the priesthood. And as a result of these demonstrations, Catholic feminists throughout America are showing their support for women's equality in the church by offering only "Monopoly" money when the collection plate is passed. The headway of the Catholic women protestors has not been remarkable, but the Catholic system nevertheless is able to accommodate such dissent. And the fact that ordination of women is now a legitimate issue under study is due to the persistent actions of Catholic women toward achieving their goals. For Mormon women the conflict is there but the conviction is lacking and the ordinary avenues for protest are blocked. Among Mormon right-wing champions of freedom, with their overriding fear of Communist infiltration, the fear of their own women dissenting presents a paradox indeed.

Whether pressure of any kind is ultimately brought to bear by Mormon women themselves, Mormonism still is based on modern revelation, the method by which the patriarchy has always retained complete control, and obviously any important change in policy for women would necessarily be accomplished by revelatory means. Certainly the granting of priesthood to women would involve such significant doctrinal alterations that it would require a major revelation. Not since the manifesto of 1890, which officially terminated the practice of plural marriage, has there been a revision of that magnitude in the Church; and whether that was a genuine revelation or an inspired decision has never been definitively settled.

Whatever its source, that change came in response to a desperate situation. Mormons frequently point out that God does not yield to social pressure, but occasionally Church authorities do. And possibly a revelation on behalf of the sisters will be forthcoming when the Saints find themselves standing alone with their all-male priesthood in a society where all other patriarchies are being dissolved. Change can only be expected to occur when the Mormons once again are so out of tune with society that their divergence constitutes a serious threat to the kingdom, which, in this case, might very well be a mass defection of women.

Because revelations have been rare in this century, and because Mormon fundamentalism has limited the possibilities for change, today's Saints have become accustomed to believing that doctrinal change is impossible. They apparently forget that just a century ago, such changes were commonplace. So flexible was Mormonism in the nineteenth century that it accomodated at least fifty doctrinal changes in the *Book of Mormon* after its first publication in 1830 and hundreds of changes were made in the *Doctrine and Covenants* as well. Clearly some Prophets have been more "fundamentalist" than others. For Mormon women, in the final analysis, the current Prophet provides the key.

Considering Mormonism's preoccupation with practical affairs, the likelihood of the Mormons acquiring an enlightened spiritual leader who is concerned more with human development than with kingdom development is remote though not altogether impossible. It is also unlikely, but there is another interesting possibility that would create the ultimate irony for women of the Church. This situation could develop through the inadvertent selection of a Mormon leader whose wife is one of the culture's strong women and one with strong feminist leanings as well. Receiving the urgent message from his wife like Caesar and Pilate, the prophet would be hastened toward that long-awaited revelation on behalf of women, thus ending a well-worn cultural tradition. The Mormon woman for the last time would be

275

forced to take the devious route through her priesthood-holding husband to make her voice heard. Until one of the above hypothetical events occurs, however, Mormon women are destined to continue the game of "Father, May I?," receiving permission to take only a series of baby steps toward solving a giant problem.

It is difficult to make a case against "I believe." People have their own special reasons for believing what they do. For many the need to adhere to a system based on theological power is compelling, an idea that has been explored extensively in literature. It is a theme of Shaw's play *St. Joan*, and the subject of Fëdor Dostoevski's magnificent essay "The Grand Inquisitor," one of the classic discussions on the nature of man. In Dostoevski's story a visitor, who is recognized as Jesus, comes to a Spanish village at the time of the Inquisition. Heretics have been burned at the stake. Jesus comes to offer the people unlimited freedom but he is confronted by the Grand Inquisitor, the Cardinal, who tells him that his coming only hinders the work of the church. In the long discussion that follows, the Inquisitor, although saddened by his own skepticism, convinces the Holy Visitor, the naive humanist, that freedom is inconsistent with the nature of mankind. The Inquisitor has concluded, in essence, that the church, in the name of happiness, has been forced to relieve mankind of the intolerable burden of his own freedom.[5]

Women especially have feared the burden of their own freedom. Women of Mormonism, and to varying degrees, women in other faiths and denominations, until now have not only accepted the security of religion, with its mystery and miracle, but have also embraced patriarchal authority as a necessary part of that religion. But of all the historical misuses of power—the rich against the poor and the strong against the weak—perhaps the most obscene has been the use of patriarchal power to control the lives of women, which is discrimination in the name of God. Extricating themselves from that patriarchal exploitation, however innocently executed, remains the most formidable task of feminists today, and they should be appropriately aided rather than resisted in that endeavor by the patriarchal leaders themselves. As an Episcopal minister sensitively observed, "Any religious denomination in the late twentieth century that is not re-evaluating the position of women in the church is not dealing realistically with the world."

On the deepest level then, feminism is a spiritual movement. Many women today, in intellectually coming to grips with feminism and religion, are choosing to accept the religious life on their own terms, with the strong belief that any move toward androgeny, integration, and the elimination of the patriarchal world view is a move toward a more creative and enlightened society.

277

NOTES

Chapter 1: MORMON WOMAN: SUBSTANCE AND MYTH

1. Edward Tullidge, *History of Salt Lake City* (Salt Lake City: Star Publishing Co., 1886), p. 438.
2. Ibid., p. 437.
3. Kate B. Carter, comp., *Our Pioneer Heritage*, 17 vols. (Salt Lake City: Daughters of the Utah Pioneers, 1958–1974), 6:426.
4. Clair Wilcox Noall, *Guardians of the Hearth* (Bountiful, Utah: Horizon Publishers, 1974), p. 127.
5. Jean Bickmore White, "Gentle Persuaders—Utah's First Woman Legislators," *Utah Historical Quarterly*, Vol. 38, Winter 1970, p. 32.
6. Edward Tullidge, *Women of Mormondom* (New York, 1877; reprint ed., Salt Lake City, 1973), p. 530.
7. Ibid.
8. Marilyn L. Warenski, Oral History Project, "Status of Women in the Mormon Culture," transcribed by Utah State Historical Society, 1974–78.

9. Mary Daly, *Beyond God the Father* (Boston: Beacon Press, 1973), pp. 122–123.

Chapter 2: WOMAN AND THE PRIESTHOOD

1. *L'Osservatore Romano,* May 1, 1975; quoted by United Press International, January 31, 1976.
2. *New York Times,* November 23, 1975.
3. *Salt Lake Tribune,* September 26, 1976.
4. Thomas F. O'Dea, *The Mormons* (Chicago: University of Chicago Press, 1957), p. 249.
5. Sterling M. McMurrin, *The Theological Foundations of the Mormon Religion* (Salt Lake City: University of Utah Press, 1965), p. 113.
6. Warenski, Status of Mormon Women Project.
7. Brigham Young and Others, *Journal of Discourses,* 25 vols. (Liverpool: 1854–1886); John Taylor, 20:359.
8. Charles W. Penrose, Latter-day Saint Conference Report, April 6, 1921, p. 198; cited in Rodney Turner, *Woman and the Priesthood* (Salt Lake City: Deseret Book Co., 1973), p. 286.
9. Young, *Journal of Discourses,* 17:119.
10. Warenski, Status of Mormon Women Project.
11. Ibid.
12. Turner, *Woman and the Priesthood,* p. 306.
13. Young, *Journal of Discourses,* 5:177.
14. Young, *Journal of Discourses,* 5:267.
15. Waldemer P. Read, "What Difference Does It Make?," paper read at Great Issues Forum, University of Utah, January 1965.
16. Joseph Smith, *History of the Church of Jesus Christ of Latter-day Saints,* Period I, Introd. and Notes by B.H. Roberts (Salt Lake City: Deseret News, 1905), III, p. 386; cited in McMurrin, *Theological Foundations of the Mormon Religion,* p. 17.
17. McMurrin, *Theological Foundations of the Mormon Religion,* p. 17.

18. Turner, *Woman and the Priesthood*, p. 285.
19. *History of the Church*, 4:602; cited in Turner, *Woman and the Priesthood*, p. 281.
20. *Teachings of the Prophet Joseph Smith*, ed. by Joseph Fielding Smith (Salt Lake City, 1938), p. 224; cited in Turner, *Woman and the Priesthood*, p. 281.
21. Young, *Journal of Discourses*, 13:155.
22. *Millenial Star*, 15:130; cited in Turner, *Woman and the Priesthood*, p. 282.
23. Warenski, Status of Mormon Women Project.
24. Jill Mulvay, "Eliza Snow and the Woman Question," Brigham Young University Studies, 16, Winter 1976, p. 264.
25. Turner, *Woman and the Priesthood*, p. 287.
26. Ibid.
27. Charles W. Penrose, Conference Records, April 6, 1921, p. 199; cited in Turner, *Woman and the Priesthood*, p. 283.
28. Sheila D. Collins, *A Different Heaven and Earth* (Valley Forge, Pa.: Judson Press, 1974), pp. 130–131.
29. Warenski, Status of Mormon Women Project.
30. Turner, *Woman and the Priesthood*, p. 283.
31. Ibid.
32. Warenski, Status of Mormon Women Project.
33. Turner, *Woman and the Priesthood*, p. 287.
34. Warenski, Status of Mormon Women Project.
35. Ibid.
36. Tom Wolfe, "The Me Decade," *New York Magazine*, August 23, 1976, p. 39.
37. McMurrin, *Theological Foundations of the Mormon Religion*, p. 112.
38. Warenski, Status of Mormon Women Project.

Chapter 3: MORMONS AND THE WORK ETHIC

1. McMurrin, *Theological Foundations of the Mormon Religion*, p. 70.
2. *Doctrine and Covenants*, 93:29.

3. McMurrin, *Theological Foundations of the Mormon Religion,* p. 29.
4. Young, *Journal of Discourses,* 12:74.
5. *Salt Lake Tribune,* October 3, 1976.
6. Young, *Journal of Discourses,* 10:131.
7. Ibid., 4:151.
8. *Salt Lake Tribune,* April 1976.
9. Susa Young Gates, *History of the Young Ladies' Mutual Improvement Association of the Church,* November 1869–June 1910 (Salt Lake City, 1911), p. 9.
10. Young, *Discourses of Brigham Young,* ed. by John A. Widtsoe (Salt Lake City, 1925), p. 462; cited in O'Dea, *The Mormons,* p. 144.
11. *Doctrine and Covenants,* 93:36.
12. *Salt Lake Tribune,* October 3, 1976.
13. *Deseret News,* Church Section, May 26, 1945, and *Improvement Era* (Salt Lake City), June 1945, p. 354.
14. *Deseret News,* April 22, 1860; cited in *A Centenary of the Relief Society* (Salt Lake City, 1942).

Chapter 4: DOUBLE DOSE OF THE DOUBLE MESSAGE

1. Thomas Monson, "Women's Movement: Liberation or Deception?," reprint from *The Ensign,* Vol. 1, No. 1, January 1971 (Salt Lake City: Mormon Church Publications), p. 77.
2. *Salt Lake Tribune,* October 5, 1974.
3. *The Ensign,* Vol. 5, February 1975, p. 4.
4. *Salt Lake Tribune,* October 6, 1974.
5. *Salt Lake Tribune,* October 3, 1974.
6. *Journal History of the Church,* December 10, 1856 (Salt Lake City: Church Historian's Office), 14th General Epistle.
7. Ibid.
8. Young, *Journal of Discourses,* 10:6.
9. Warenski, Status of Mormon Women Project.
10. Ibid.
11. *Salt Lake Tribune,* October 1, 1975.

12. Turner, *Woman and the Priesthood*, p. 289.
13. Elizabeth Cady Stanton, *Eighty Years or More: Reminiscences 1815–1897* (New York: Schocken Books, 1973), p. 286.
14. Warenski, Status of Mormon Women Project.
15. Rodney W. Burgoyne, M.D., and Robert H. Burgoyne, M.D., "Conflicts Secondary to Overt Paradoxes in Belief Systems—the Mormon Woman Example," *Journal of Operational Psychiatry*, Vol. VIII, No. 2, 1977, p. 39.
16. Warenski, Status of Mormon Women Project.
17. Ibid.
18. Ibid.
19. Ibid.

Chapter 5: RELIEF SOCIETY: SISTERHOOD OF THE BROTHERHOOD

1. Relief Society Minutes, March 17, 1842; cited in *A Centenary of the Relief Society, 1842–1942*, comp. by General Board of the Relief Society (Salt Lake City, 1942), p. 15
2. *Relief Society Magazine*, March 1919, 6:129; cited in *A Centenary of the Relief Society*, p. 14.
3. Relief Society Minutes, March 17, 1842; cited in *A Centenary of the Relief Society*, p. 15.
4. *Documentary History of the Church*, Vol. 4 (Salt Lake City), pp. 606–607; cited in *A Centenary of the Relief Society*, p. 16.
5. Ibid.
6. *Relief Society Magazine*, 6:129; cited in *A Centenary of the Relief Society*, p. 14.
7. Gates, *History of the Young Ladies' Mutual Improvement Association of the Church*, pp. 8–9.
8. Young, *Journal of Discourses*, 5:176–177.
9. Ibid., 16:21.
10. Leonard Arrington, "Economic Role of Mormon Women," *Western Humanities Review*, Vol. 9, No. 2, Spring 1955, p. 146.
11. Ibid.

12. Gates, *History of the Young Ladies' Mutual Improvement Association of the Church,* pp. 8–9; cited in Arrington, "Economic Role of Mormon Women," p. 149.
13. Young, *Journal of Discourses,* 14:103.
14. Arrington, "Economic Role of Mormon Women," p. 148.
15. Gates, *History of the Young Ladies' Mutual Improvement Association of the Church,* pp. 9–10; cited in Arrington, "Economic Role of Mormon Women," p. 149.
16. *Journal History of the Church,* October 4, 1876; cited in Arrington, "Economic Role of Mormon Women," p. 151.
17. *Woman's Exponent,* III (1875), p. 157; cited in Arrington, "Economic Role of Mormon Women," p. 152.
18. *A Centenary of the Relief Society,* p. 11.
19. Margaret Schow Potter, "The History of Sericulture in Utah" (master's thesis, Oregon State College, 1949), p. 29; cited in Arrington, "Economic Role of Mormon Women," p. 154.
20. *Relief Society Magazine,* February 1915, p. 47; cited in *A Centenary of the Relief Society,* p. 72.
21. Clair Wilcox Noall, "Utah's Pioneer Women Doctors," *Improvement Era,* XLII (1939), pp. 16–17; cited in Arrington, "Economic Role of Mormon Women," p. 162.
22. *Woman's Exponent,* II (1873), p. 35; cited in *A Centenary of the Relief Society,* p. 45.
23. Young, *Journal of Discourses,* 5:190–191.
24. Ibid., 9:307.
25. Ibid., 19:73.
26. *A Centenary of the Relief Society,* p. 18.
27. Rodello Hunter, *A Daughter of Zion* (New York: Alfred A. Knopf, 1972), p. 268.
28. Warenski, Status of Mormon Women Project.
29. Ibid.
30. Ibid.
31. Ibid.
32. Ibid.
33. *A Centenary of the Relief Society,* p. 9.
34. Ibid., p. 7.

35. Warenski, Status of Mormon Women Project.
36. Ibid.

Chapter 6: POLYGAMOUS SUFFRAGETTES

1. Tullidge, *History of Salt Lake City*, p. 433, quoting from "Biography of William Hooper," *Phrenological Journal*, November 1871.
2. O'Dea, *The Mormons*, pp. 61–62.
3. Fawn M. Brodie, *No Man Knows My History* (New York: Alfred A. Knopf, 1945), p. 447.
4. Young, *Journal of Discourses*, 17:159.
5. Mark Twain, *Roughing It* (Hartford, 1872), pp. 117–118.
6. Richard F. Burton, *The City of the Saints and Across the Rock Mountains to California*, edited by Fawn M. Brodie (New York: Alfred A. Knopf, 1963); cited in Gail Farr Casterline, *In the Toils or Onward for Zion* (Utah State University, 1974), p. 57.
7. Jean Bickmore White, "Gentle Persuaders—Utah's First Woman Legislators," *Utah Historical Quarterly*, 38, Winter 1970, p. 45.
8. Helen Mar Whitney, *Why We Practice Plural Marriage* (Salt Lake City: Juvenile Instructor Press, 1884), p. 53.
9. Ellis Shipp Musser, comp. and ed., *The Early Autobiography and Diary of Ellis Reynolds Shipp, M.D.* (Salt Lake City: Deseret News Press, 1962), p. 162.
10. S. George Ellsworth, ed., *Dear Ellen: Two Mormon Women and Their Letters* (Tanner Trust Fund, University of Utah Library), p. 42.
11. Ibid., p. 4.
12. Young, *Journal of Discourses*, 4:55.
13. Ibid.
14. Ibid., p. 57.
15. Tullidge, *History of Salt Lake City*, p. 435.
16. Ibid.
17. Ibid.

18. T.A. Larson, "Woman's Suffrage in Utah," *Utah Historical Quarterly*, Vol. 38, Winter 1970, p. 20.
19. Tullidge, *Women of Mormondom*, p. 502.
20. Ibid.
21. Ibid., p. 503.
22. Ibid.
23. Reynolds vs. United States (Supreme Court of the United States), 98 U.S. 145 (1878); cited in O'Dea, *The Mormons*, pp. 108–109.
24. *Woman's Exponent*, January 1873, p. 46; cited in Casterline, *In the Toils or Onward for Zion*, p. 120.
25. Tullidge, *Women of Mormondom*, pp. 507–508.
26. United States Congress, House of Representatives, "Suffrage in Utah: Memorial of the New York Suffrage Society," *House Misc. Dec. 95*, 42nd Congress, February 17, 1873; cited in Casterline, p. 128.
27. *Woman's Exponent*, May 1, 1879, reprint of Elizabeth Cady Stanton letter, p. 240.
28. Stanton, *Eighty Years or More: Reminiscences 1815–1897*, p. 285.
29. Tullidge, *Women of Mormondom*, p. 501

Chapter 7: THE HOTDOG INVASION

1. Margaret I. Miller and Helene Linker, "Equal Rights Amendment Campaigns in California and Utah," *Society Magazine*, Vol. II, No. 4, May/June 1974, pp. 42–43.
2. Ibid., p. 50.
3. Ibid.
4. Ibid., p. 49.
5. O'Dea, *The Mormons*, p. 173.
6. *Salt Lake Tribune*, November 15, 1975.
7. Ibid., 1966.
8. ERA File, Governor's Committee on the Status of Women, Utah State Capitol Building.
9. Ibid.

10. Ibid.
11. Ibid.

Chapter 8: SHE IS MY PRINCESS

1. Suzanna Mae Grua, "Equal Rights Amendment," printed privately (Salt Lake City, 1974).
2. *Salt Lake Tribune,* December 14, 1974.
3. Warenski, Status of Mormon Women Project.
4. *Salt Lake Tribune,* January 14, 1975.
5. Ibid., January 23, 1975.
6. Warenski, Status of Mormon Women Project.
7. Ibid.
8. *Salt Lake Tribune,* April 18, 1975.
9. Estelle Neff Caldwell, "Susa Young Gates," *Latter-day Saint Biographical Encyclopedia* (Salt Lake City, 1942), p. 629.
10. Ibid.
11. R. Paul Cracroft, "Susa Young Gates, Her Life and Literary Work" (master's thesis, University of Utah, 1951), p. 13.
12. Ibid.
13. Ibid., p. 15.
14. *Salt Lake Tribune,* April 21, 1975.

Chapter 9: UNMARRIED IN A MARRIED CHURCH

1. Whitney, *Why We Practice Plural Marriage,* p. 10.
2. Young, *Journal of Discourses,* 4:56.
3. Whitney, *Why We Practice Plural Marriage,* p. 52.
4. Ibid., p. 14.
5. Ibid., p. 46.
6. Young, *Journal of Discourses,* 12:262.
7. Whitney, *Why We Practice Plural Marriage,* p. 31
8. Ibid., p. 41.
9. *Salt Lake Tribune,* June 22, 1974.
10. Ibid.
11. Ibid., June 28, 1975.
12. Ibid.

13. Ibid.
14. Ibid.
15. Warenski, Status of Mormon Women Project.
16. Ibid.
17. Ibid.
18. Ibid.
19. Ibid.
20. *Salt Lake Tribune,* October 1, 1975.
21. *Deseret News,* May 10, 1975.
22. *Salt Lake Tribune,* October 1, 1975.
23. Ibid., June 22, 1974.
24. Carol Clark, *A Singular Life* (Salt Lake City: Deseret Book Co. Press, 1974), p. 38.
25. Ibid., p. 56.
26. Bruce R. McConkie, *Mormon Doctrine* (Salt Lake City: Deseret Book Co. Press), p. 97.
27. Joseph Fielding Smith, *Doctrines of Salvation,* Vol. II (Salt Lake City: Bookcraft, 1955), p. 76.

Chapter 10: REVELATION OR REVOLUTION

1. Leonard Swidler, "Jesus Was a Feminist," *Catholic World,* Vol. 212, No. 1270, January 1971, pp. 177–183.
2. Sigmund Freud, *Civilization and Its Discontents* (New York: W.W. Norton, The Norton Library), pp 62–63.
3. Dennis Michael Quinn, *The Mormon Hierarchy, 1832–1932: An American Elite* (New Haven: Yale University, 1976), p. 283.
4. Warenski, Status of Mormon Women Project.
5. Fëdor Dostoevski, "The Grand Inquisitor on the Nature of Man," taken from *The Brothers Karamazov* (New York: Bobbs-Merrill, 1948), pp. 21–44.

SELECTED
BIBLIOGRAPHY

Beeton, Beverly *Woman Suffrage in the American West* (Salt Lake City: University of Utah, 1977).

Brodie, Fawn M. *No Man Knows My History: The Life of Joseph Smith* (New York: Alfred A. Knopf, 1945).

Bushman, Claudia *Mormon Sisters: Women in Early Utah* (Boston: Mormon Sisters, Inc., 1976).

Casterline, Gail Farr *In the Toils or Onward for Zion: Images of the Mormon Woman: 1852–1890* (Logan, Utah: Utah State University, 1974).

Collins, Sheila D. *A Different Heaven and Earth* (Valley Forge, Pa.: Judson Press, 1974).

Daly, Mary *Beyond God the Father* (Boston: Beacon Press, 1973). *The Church and the Second Sex*, Revised Edition (New York: Harper & Row, 1975).

Dostoevski, Fëdor *The Grand Inquisitor on the Nature of Man* (New York: Bobbs-Merrill, 1948).

Ellsworth, S. George *Dear Ellen: Two Mormon Women and Their Letters* (Salt Lake City: Tanner Trust Fund, University of Utah Library, 1974).

Ericksen, E.E. *The Psychological and Ethical Aspects of Mormon Group Life* (Salt Lake City: University of Utah Press, 1975).

Hume, David *Dialogues Concerning Natural Religion* (New York: Hafner Publishing Co., 1948).

Hunter, Rodello *A Daughter of Zion* (New York: Alfred A. Knopf, 1972).

Kane, Elizabeth Wood *Twelve Mormon Homes* (Salt Lake City: Tanner Trust Fund, University of Utah Library, 1974).

McMurrin, Sterling M. *Theological Foundations of the Mormon Church* (Salt Lake City: University of Utah Press, 1969).

Noall, Claire Wilcox *Guardians of the Hearth: Utah's Pioneer Midwives and Women Doctors* (Bountiful, Utah : Horizon Publishers, 1974).

O'Dea, Thomas F. *The Mormons* (Chicago: University of Chicago Press, 1957).

Peterson, Charles S. *Take Up Your Mission: Mormon Colonizing Along the Little Colorado River* (Tucson: University of Arizona Press, 1973).

Reuther, Rosemary *Liberation Theology* (New York: Paulist Press, 1972).

Rogers, Lewis M., and Monson, Charles H. *And More About God* (Salt Lake City: University of Utah Press, 1969).

Stanton, Elizabeth Cady *The Woman's Bible* (New York: Arno Press, New York Times Co., 1972).

Stegner, Wallace *The Gathering of Zion* (New York: McGraw-Hill, 1964).

Stendahl, Krister *The Bible and the Role of Women* (Philadelphia: Fortress Press, 1966).

Tanner, Annie Clark *A Mormon Mother* (Salt Lake City: Tanner Trust Fund, University of Utah Library).

Tillich, Paul *Systematic Theology* (Chicago: University of Chicago Press, 1951).

INDEX

291